Galley
SOUPS FOR ALL SEASONS

MAYFLOWER BOOKS, INC., U.S.A.
575 Lexington Avenue
New York, New York 10022

CONTENTS

BOUQUET GARNI

A bouquet garni of herbs and spices is for seasoning stew or soup. The herbs are tied together or into a cheesecloth bag for easy removal.

- 1 t. dried parsley
- 1½ t. dried thyme
- 1¼ t. dried marjoram
- ½ t. sage
- ½ t. dried savory
- ¼ t. bay leaf
- 1½ t. celery seed
- 5 peppercorns

Crush together herbs and spices. Pack into a small bag made from several layers of cheesecloth. Tightly tie the bag shut with string. Add the garni while simmering the ingredients for any soup. Take out before serving and discard. In bouquet garni, the amount of any ingredient can be increased as desired according to personal tastes.

The Stock Pot

HERB BOUQUET

In an herb bouquet, herbs are tied together, or put tied into a cheesecloth, for seasoning soup or stew.

- 3 or 4 sprigs parsley
- 1 sprig thyme
- 1 bay leaf
- 1 sprig dill

Tie herbs together and drop into soup, stews, braised dishes and sauces as flavoring. Or, they can be crushed and tied in a cheesecloth bag. Take out before serving.

CHICKEN BROTH

4 to 5 lb. stewing chicken, cut up
1¼ qt. hot water
2 t. salt
5 3-inch pieces of celery with leaves
3 small carrots
2 medium onions
1 large tomato, quartered

Place chicken, reserving liver, in large stewing kettle. Add water, salt and vegetables. Cover and bring to a boil; reduce heat. Uncover and remove foam. Simmer tightly covered 2 to 3 hours, adding the liver for the last 15 minutes. Remove chicken from broth. Strain the broth through a cheesecloth-lined colander. Cool slightly. Skim off the fat that rises to the top. If broth is too rich, add more water. Refrigerate until needed. Makes about 1 quart broth.

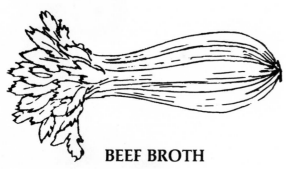

BEEF BROTH

4 lbs. beef soup bones, small and meaty
2½ qts. cold water
1 t. salt
1 bay leaf
1 medium onion, peeled
2 whole cloves
5 whole peppercorns
1 carrot, pared
1 stalk celery with leaves
2 sprigs parsley

Put bones, water and remaining ingredients into a large soup kettle. Do not cover. Simmer for 3 hours, then strain. Use the meat in hash or sandwiches. Remove fat from broth by refrigerating overnight, then skimming fat off top. Serve hot with crackers or use as a base for other soups.

FISH STOCK

1 qt. water
1 T. salt
1 lb. fish trimmings (head, bones, skin, fins and tail)

Place all ingredients in a large soup kettle. Bring to a boil. Cover and simmer for 30 minutes. Strain liquid through a colander covered with 2 thicknesses of cheesecloth. If not to be used at once, cool and refrigerate. Can be frozen. To be used as directed in recipes for fish soups.

BROWN STOCK

¼ c. fat
3 lbs. lean meat, chuck or blade
1 soup bone
3 qts. water
1½ T. salt
  Herb bouquet
1 medium onion
2 whole cloves
5 carrots, peeled and cubed
2 turnips, peeled and cubed
1 parsnip, peeled and cubed
4 leeks, chopped (white part only)
3 celery stalks with leaves, diced
1 onion, diced

In a large skillet brown meat and bone in fat, browning on all sides. Place in a large soup kettle. Add water, salt and herb bouquet. Insert cloves into center of onion, then add onion to pot. Bring to a boil, then reduce heat. Cover and simmer 4 hours. Add vegetables. Add water as necessary while cooking. Simmer 1½ hours. Strain through a fine sieve. Meat and vegetables may be served as desired. If stock is to be used at once, skim fat from cooled broth and reheat. Serve with toast. Stock can be stored in covered container for future use. When cool, remove hardened fat. Makes about 2½ quarts of stock.

WHITE STOCK

3 lbs. veal breast
1 veal shank
5 or 6 bony pieces of chicken
3 qts. water
1½ t. salt
5 carrots, diced
2 turnips, diced
1 parsnip, diced
4 leeks (white part only)
3 stalks celery with leaves, diced
1 large onion, diced
1 medium onion
2 whole cloves
  Herb bouquet

In large soup kettle, combine veal, veal shank and chicken pieces. Add water and salt. Cover. Bring to a boil. Reduce heat and simmer 4 hours. Prepare vegetables, inserting cloves into middle of onion. Add vegetables to pot with seasonings. Simmer an additional 1½ hour. Remove from heat, and strain through a sieve. Meat and vegetables may be served as desired. When broth is cool, put in refrigerator to chill. Remove hardened fat. Store in tightly covered container. Makes about 2½ quarts stock.

BOUILLON

2 qts. brown stock
2 egg whites, slightly beaten
2 crushed egg shells

In a large soup kettle, stir into the brown stock the egg whites and crushed egg shells. Heat slowly to a boil, stirring constantly. Remove from heat. Cool 25 minutes. Strain through a colander covered with 2 thicknesses of cheesecloth. Refrigerate until needed. Can be frozen.

VEGETABLE STOCK

4 c. water
2 c. chopped celery stalks and leaves
1 large onion, chopped
½ c. chopped cabbage
1 large carrot, diced
6 peppercorns
1 bay leaf
½ t. salt
1 6-oz. can tomato juice

Combine all ingredients in a large saucepan. Simmer, covered, for about 1 hour. Strain. Use immediately or store in refrigerator until needed. Makes 6 cups.

HAM STOCK

1 ham bone, meaty
2 qts. water
1 small onion
3 celery tops
2 parsley sprigs
1 bay leaf, broken
6 peppercorns
  Salt to taste

Combine all ingredients except salt. Bring to a boil then reduce the heat and cover. Simmer for 2 hours or longer. Season with salt. Strain, cool and chill. Skim off fat. Use recipe as a soup or stew base. Can be refrigerated in airtight containers for up to 1 week, or frozen for up to 6 months. Makes about 6 cups.

CONSOMMÉ

2 qts. white stock, cold
2 egg whites, slightly beaten
2 crushed egg shells
4 t. water

In a large kettle stir into the cold white stock, the egg whites and the egg shells mixed with the water. Slowly heat to a boil, stirring constantly. Remove from heat. Cool 25 minutes. Strain through a colander covered with 2 layers of cheesecloth. Refrigerate broth until needed. Can be frozen.

Bean, Lentil, Pea and Pasta Soup

LIMA BEAN SOUP

1 c. dried lima beans
2 lbs. meaty veal bones, shoulder or neck
3 carrots, peeled and diced
¼ c. whole barley
2 onions, cut in chunks
3 fresh tomatoes, quartered, *or*
  2 c. tomato juice
2 bay leaves
  Salt and pepper to taste

Soak beans overnight in 2 cups water. Next day, add to the beans, veal bones, bay leaves and 2 additional cups water or stock. Bring to a boil. Reduce heat and simmer for 1½ hours or until beans are soft. Add rest of ingredients. Simmer for another hour or until carrots are soft. Serve hot. Serves 4 to 6.

BEAN SOUP WITH NOODLES

1 c. dried white beans
1 qt. water
1 t. salt
1 ham bone
¼ c. diced carrots
¼ c. diced celery
¼ c. chopped onion
1 bay leaf
  Water to cover
½ c. broken lasagne noodles
  Salt and pepper to taste

Soak beans in salted water overnight. Drain. In soup kettle combine beans, ham bone, vegetables and bay leaf. Add enough cold water to cover. Bring to a boil. Skim froth from surface and reduce the heat. Cover and simmer for 1 hour and 30 minutes or until beans are tender. Add more water as needed to keep broth covering beans. Discard ham bone and bay leaf. Cut off any meat left on the bone. Cool soup slightly. Puree half the beans in a blender. Pour them back into the soup kettle; add the meat. Bring soup to a boil, then add the broken noodles. Cook for an additional 10 minutes or until noodles are tender. Add salt and pepper. Ladle into soup bowls and sprinkle with Parmesan cheese. Serves 4 to 6.

HAM AND NOODLE SOUP

1 lb. cooked ham, diced
1 4-oz. pkg. bow-tie egg noodles
  Vegetable oil
1 qt. chicken broth
1 9-oz. pkg. frozen French-style green beans

Prepare noodles according to package directions. Drain well and blot dry with paper towels. Heat about 1 inch oil in heavy skillet to 370°. Fry cooked noodles for about 5 minutes or until golden brown on both sides. Drain on paper towels. In soup kettle combine the broth, ham and green beans to boiling. Reduce heat and simmer for 15 minutes or until beans are tender. Add fried noodles and serve at once to retain crispness of noodles. Serves 4.

ESCAROLE SOUP

8 c. water
1 c. dried pea beans
2 T. vegetable oil
3 medium onions, chopped
1 large green pepper, chopped
2 cloves garlic, crushed
1 meaty ham bone
1 t. salt
¼ t. pepper
1 bay leaf
4 medium potatoes, peeled and diced
1 head escarole, chopped

In a large kettle, bring water and beans to a boil and boil for 2 minutes. Remove from heat. Cover and let stand for 1 hour. Do not drain. Heat oil in skillet and sauté onions, green pepper and crushed garlic until lightly browned. Stir into the beans. Add ham bone and seasonings. Bring to a boil, then reduce the heat and simmer for 1½ hours. Add potatoes and escarole and cook an additional 10 minutes or until potatoes are done. Cut the meat from the bone; add it to the soup before serving. Serves 8.

Pictured opposite
Soup with Noodles

LEAFY BEAN SOUP

1 medium onion, chopped
1 clove garlic, minced
2 T. butter or margarine
2 14-oz. cans chicken broth
1 bay leaf
1 ½-lb. bunch fresh spinach
1 1-lb. can white kidney beans or
garbanzos
Salt and pepper to taste
Parmesan cheese for garnish

In a Dutch oven or heavy soup kettle, sauté the onion and garlic over medium heat until soft and golden, about 6 minutes. Add chicken broth and bay leaf. Cover and simmer for 10 minutes. Discard spinach stems and wash leaves thoroughly. Stack leaves and slice crosswise into ¼-inch strips. Set aside. After broth has simmered, add the beans and juice. Add spinach and simmer for 5 minutes, adding salt and pepper. Remove bay leaf and serve at once with cheese. Serves 4 to 6.

MUSHROOM AND BARLEY SOUP

1 c. dried lima beans, large
3 T. barley
8 c. water or stock
1 lb. chopped soup meat
3 marrow bones
2 T. dried mushrooms or 1 4-oz. can
mushroom bits and pieces
1 large onion, sliced
2 stalks celery, diced
2 T. dried parsley or 6 fresh parsley sprigs
1 c. diced carrots
½ t. dill weed
½ t. celery salt
1 t. salt

Place washed beans and barley in large soup kettle with water or stock. Add remaining ingredients. Bring to a boil. Reduce heat and cover. Simmer for 2 hours or until beans are soft. Serve with meat and some of the marrow from the bones with each bowl of soup. Serves 8.

BAKED BEAN SOUP

1 T. bacon grease
1 medium onion, sliced
1 small clove garlic, minced
1 small green pepper, chopped
1 c. chopped tomato, fresh or canned
2 c. consommé
2 c. baked beans
1 stalk celery, cut up
½ t. chopped parsley
1 bay leaf
Salt and pepper
¼ c. Madeira or sherry
Lemon slices dusted with
paprika for garnish

Melt bacon fat in small soup kettle. Sauté onion, garlic and green pepper until onion is golden. Add tomato, consommé, baked beans, celery and parsley and seasonings. Bring to a boil; lower the heat and simmer for 30 minutes. Cool slightly. Puree the mixture in a blender. Reheat. Add the Madeira or sherry. Garnish with the lemon slices. Serves 4 to 6.

LENTIL SOUP WITH FRANKFURTERS

2 large onions, chopped
1 celery stalk, diced
1 leek, sliced
1 medium potato, peeled and cubed
3 slices bacon, diced
1 T. butter
1 c. lentils
1 carrot, diced
4 frankfurters, thickly sliced
Salt to taste
1 T. catsup
3 qts. water or chicken broth

Place onions, celery, leek, potatoes, diced bacon and butter in a heavy kettle. Sauté until soft, but not brown. Wash and drain lentils. Add them to potatoes with carrots, sliced frankfurters, salt, catsup and water or chicken broth. Bring to a boil. Lower heat and simmer, covered, for 3 hours or until lentils are soft. Add more water as needed. (Recipe can be prepared in crock pot or slow cooker according to manufacturer's directions.) Serves 8.

VEGETARIAN BLACK BEAN SOUP

1 c. black beans
4 c. water
3 bay leaves
2 onions, chopped
2 garlic cloves
¼ t. dry mustard
1½ t. chili powder
Salt to taste

Combine all ingredients. Bring to a boil. Reduce heat and simmer for 1½ hours, or until beans are tender. Cool slightly. Puree until smooth. Add salt to taste. Heat and serve. Serves 4.

CHICK PEA AND CABBAGE SOUP

2 T. vegetable oil
2 cloves garlic, minced
1 slice bread, diced in ¾" pieces
2 T. chopped parsley
1 large potato, peeled and diced
4 c. cooked chick peas, drained, or
　 2 15-oz. cans chick peas, drained
1 large tomato, chopped
1 bay leaf
4 c. shredded cabbage (½ head)
6 c. water
　 Salt to taste
½ lb. spinach, chopped

Heat oil in small skillet. Sauté garlic and bread until garlic is golden. Remove from heat. Add parsley. In large soup kettle, combine garlic mixture with remaining ingredients except spinach. Bring to a boil, then reduce heat and cook until the potato is done, about 15 to 20 minutes. The bread will soften, but this will thicken the soup. About 5 minutes before serving, add the spinach. Serves 6.

LENTIL WIENER SOUP

½ lb. dry lentils
8 c. cold water
4 strips bacon
½ c. finely chopped celery
¼ c. finely chopped onion
2 T. flour
　 Salt and pepper to taste
½ c. tomato paste or ½ c. sieved tomatoes
6 to 8 wieners

Soak lentils overnight. Next day, drain and add fresh water. Simmer for 2 hours. Chop bacon and fry until crisp. Remove the bacon. Sauté the celery and onion in the bacon fat. Stir in the flour and cook for about 3 minutes. Add to lentils with the bacon. Stir in seasonings and tomatoes or tomato paste. Cook for 30 minutes. Peel and cut wieners in ¼-inch slices. Sauté a few minutes in butter; add to soup. Cook an additional 15 minutes. Serve hot. Serves 8.

BEAN AND CORN SOUP

1 c. white beans
4 c. water or milk
1 medium onion, chopped
2 cloves garlic
1 t. turmeric
1 t. cumin
2 c. corn
　 Salt to taste

Add beans, onion, garlic and spices to water in soup kettle. When tender, cool slightly. Puree in blender. Add corn. Salt to taste. Reheat and serve. Serves 4 to 6.

LENTIL AND BARLEY SOUP

2½ c. chicken or beef stock
½ c. diced carrots
½ c. diced onion
½ T. paprika
1 c. cooked brown or red lentils
1 c. cooked barley
¼ t. cumin
1 c. yogurt

Combine all ingredients except the yogurt. Simmer for one hour or until vegetables are soft. Just before serving, stir in yogurt. Serves 6.

9

SENATE BEAN SOUP

1 lb. dried beans (navy, pea or
   great northern)
   Water
1 meaty ham bone
3 medium potatoes, peeled and diced
1 large onion, chopped
1 c. diced celery
1 c. diced carrot
2 cloves garlic, minced
   Salt and pepper to taste

In a large soup kettle, soak the beans over-night in 2 quarts water. Next morning, add 2 more quarts water and ham bone. Bring to a boil. Reduce heat and cover. Simmer for 2 hours or until beans are tender. Add pota-toes, onions, celery, carrot and garlic. Simmer 1 hour longer. Cut meat off bone and add to soup. If desired, mash beans and vegetables to thicken the soup. Season. Makes about 4 quarts. Can be frozen.

SAUSAGE BEAN POTATO SOUP

1 c. dried lima beans
5 c. water
¼ lb. sausage
1 small onion, chopped
1 c. milk
1 c. diced potato
1 t. salt
½ t. turmeric, optional
⅛ t. pepper

In a saucepan, bring beans and water to a boil. Remove from heat. Cover and let stand for 1 hour. Sauté sausage and onion in a skillet until lightly browned. Drain, and add to beans with 2 cups water. Cover and simmer for 2 hours or until beans are tender. Add milk, potato and seasonings. Cover and simmer over low heat for 20 minutes or until potatoes are done. Makes about 2 quarts.

WINE RED KIDNEY BEAN SOUP

1 c. dried red kidney beans
4 c. water
1 onion, chopped
½ t. salt
¾ c. red wine

Simmer beans and onions in boiling water until tender. Mash half the beans. Add salt and wine. Simmer 20 minutes more. Serve hot. Serves 4.

BEAN SOUP WITH SALT PORK

1 lb. dried beans, navy, pea or
   great northern
1 qt. cold water
½ lb. salt pork or bacon sliced in 2-inch
   pieces
1 medium onion, chopped
1 stalk celery, diced
1 whole clove
1 bay leaf
1 t. salt
½ t. pepper

Let beans soak overnight. Place beans and soaking water in large soup kettle. Add salt pork or bacon, onion and celery. Bring to a boil; simmer, covered, for 2 hours, adding more water as needed. When beans are soft, add seasonings. Before serving, remove bay leaf. Serve with corn bread, a green salad and dessert.

SPLIT PEA SOUP WITH HAM

2 c. split peas
3 qts. cold water
1 ham bone plus 1 c. diced ham
1 small onion
¼ c. diced celery
1 t. salt
½ t. pepper

Soak peas overnight in enough water to cover. In the morning, add 3 quarts cold water to ham bone. Add drained peas, celery, onion, seasoning, and diced ham. Heat to boiling. Reduce heat and simmer slowly for about 4 hours or until peas are soft. Add more water as needed. Serve hot. Serves 4.

Pictured opposite
Split Pea Soup with H

Chowder and Gumbo

MANHATTAN FISH CHOWDER

1 small onion, minced
2 T. fat or salad oil
1 large potato, peeled and diced
1 c. diced celery
1¼ c. cooked or canned tomatoes
　　Salt and pepper to taste
1½ c. whole kernel corn
1 c. codfish, cooked and flaked
　　Hard roll, sliced
　　Grated Parmesan cheese for garnish

Heat oil in skillet. Sauté onion until tender. Add potato, celery, tomatoes and seasoning. Simmer for 15 minutes. Add corn and fish. Heat to boiling. Slice roll. Toast. Place a slice in each soup bowl. Ladle chowder over bread. Sprinkle with cheese. Serves 4 to 6.

GUMBO FILÉ

1 pt. oysters
1 stewing chicken, cut up
2 t. salt
1½ t. monosodium glutamate
1 small onion
3 sprigs parsley
2 3-inch pieces celery with leaves
1 bay leaf
2 or 3 peppercorns
1 c. diced, cooked ham
1 c. chopped onion
½ t. salt
2 T. chicken fat
⅛ t. pepper
⅛ t. cayenne
2 T. filé powder

Drain oysters, reserving liquid. Refrigerate until needed. In large saucepan, simmer chicken in water to cover with salt and monosodium glutamate, onion, parsley, celery, bay leaf and peppercorns for 2 to 3 hours, or chicken is done. Remove chicken from broth. Strain broth and cool slightly. Remove skin and bones from cooled chicken. Dice chicken meat and set aside. Sauté onion and ham in chicken fat until onion is transparent. Add chicken broth, oyster liquid, diced chicken, pepper and cayenne. Simmer for 1 hour. About 10 minutes before serving, add oysters. Cook until the edges of oysters begin to curl. Remove from heat. Add ½ cup of the liquid with filé powder. Add mixture to soup, stirring thoroughly. Serve gumbo over mounds of rice. Serves 6 to 8. *Note*: Filé powder should always be added after the soup has been removed from the heat. If cooked, the gumbo will become stringy and unpalatable. Serves 6.

FISH CHOWDER

¼ c. diced salt pork
¾ c. sliced onions
2 c. hot water
2 c. sliced potatoes
2 or 3 lbs. cod or haddock, cut in chunks
2½ t. salt
　　Dash of pepper
1 c. evaporated milk
3 c. fresh milk

Fry salt pork in a heavy kettle until crisp and delicately browned. Add onions and sauté until light brown. Add water and potatoes. Cook 5 minutes. Add fish and cook an additional 10 minutes or until fish flakes easily with a fork. Add pepper and milk. Reheat. Serves 6.

TOMATO CORN CHOWDER

1 10¾-oz. can tomato soup
1 soup can milk
½ c. cream-style corn
¼ t. curry powder
1 t. sugar
¼ t. salt

Heat soup and milk in a saucepan. Add the corn, curry powder, sugar and salt. Heat to boiling. Serve with croutons. Serves 4.

DUTCH BROWN POTATO CHOWDER

    5 potatoes, diced
    2 T. butter
    5 T. flour
    ½ t. salt
      Dash of pepper
    ½ t. minced parsley
    1 t. butter

Cook potatoes until tender. Add additional water to make a quart. In a frying pan, melt butter. Add flour, stirring to avoid burning, and cook until flour is golden brown. Add to the potatoes and water. Stir until creamy, but do not smash the potatoes. Simmer until soup thickens. Add parsley, seasoning and butter. Serve hot.

FISH MULLIGAN

    2 lbs. fish, cut in chunks
    4 potatoes, peeled and cubed
    2 onions, skinned and sliced
    6 cups water
    ½ c. raw rice
    1 green pepper, seeded and cut in chunks
    2 to 4 slices of bacon, diced
    2 carrots, peeled and sliced
    2 stalks celery, cleaned and diced

Combine fish, potatoes, onions and water. Bring to a boil and add rice, green pepper, bacon, carrots and celery. Again bring to a boil. Reduce heat. Cover and simmer for ½ hour or until all the vegetables are tender. Add seasonings and serve with crusty rolls. Serves 4 to 6.

QUICK CHICKEN CHOWDER

    ½ c. chopped onion
    2 T. butter or margarine
    2 10¾-oz. cans chicken noodle soup
    1 soup can water
    2 c. cream-style corn
    ⅔ c. evaporated milk
    ¼ t. pepper
    2 T. chopped chives

Sauté onion in butter until soft. Stir in remaining ingredients except chives. Heat to boiling. Pour into soup bowls. Sprinkle with chives. Serves 6.

NEW ENGLAND VEGETABLE CHOWDER

    ¼ c. butter or margarine
    1 small onion, chopped
    1 green pepper, chopped
    1 c. diced celery
    1 c. diced carrot
    1½ c. whole kernel corn
    1 c. grated cabbage
    1 c. peas
    ½ t. salt
    ⅛ t. pepper
    2 T. chopped parsley
    4 c. milk
      Grated American cheese for garnish

Melt butter in heavy kettle. Add onion, green pepper and celery. Sauté until limp. Add rest of the vegetables and seasoning. Add enough water to cover. Cook 1 hour. Stir in milk and parsley. Ladle into soup bowls. Sprinkle with cheese. Serves 4 to 6.

SOUTHERN TURKEY GUMBO

    3 lbs. turkey wings, disjointed
    3 c. chicken broth or water
    1 c. celery tops
    2 bay leaves
    1 T. salt
    2 T. butter or margarine
    1 large onion, sliced
    1 medium green pepper, coarsely chopped
    2 1-lb. cans tomatoes
    ½ t. hot pepper sauce
    ⅓ c. uncooked rice
    1 10-oz. pkg. frozen cut okra
    1 t. filé powder
      Chopped parsley

In a heavy 4-quart kettle, combine turkey wings with broth or water, celery tops, bay leaves and salt. Simmer for 1 hour, adding more water if necessary. Strain and remove meat from bones. Add water, if necessary, to make 1¼ cups broth. Put broth and meat back in the kettle. Sauté onion and green pepper in butter. Add to turkey and broth with tomatoes, pepper sauce, and rice. Simmer for about 30 minutes. Add okra and simmer an additional 6 to 8 minutes. Remove from heat and stir in filé powder. Sprinkle with parsley. Serves 4 to 6.

CATFISH GUMBO

1 lb. skinned catfish fillets
½ c. chopped celery
½ c. chopped green peppers
½ c. chopped onion
1 clove garlic, finely chopped
¼ c. melted fat or oil
2 beef bouillon cubes
2 c. boiling water
1 1-lb. can tomatoes
1 10-oz. pkg. frozen okra, sliced
2 t. salt
¼ t. pepper
¼ t. thyme
1 bay leaf
Dash of liquid hot pepper sauce
1½ c. hot cooked rice.

Cut fish in one inch pieces. Cook celery, green pepper, onion and garlic in fat until tender. Dissolve bouillon cubes in hot water. Add tomatoes, okra and seasonings. Cover. Simmer for 30 minutes. Add fish. Cover and simmer for an additional 15 minutes or until fish flakes easily with fork. Remove bay leaf. Place ¼ cup rice in each of 6 soup bowls. Fill with hot gumbo. Serves 6.

CRAB SHRIMP GUMBO

2 T. butter or margarine
¾ c. chopped onion
½ c. chopped green pepper
2 stalks celery, chopped
¼ lb. cooked, diced ham
1 clove garlic, finely minced
6 ripe tomatoes, peeled and chopped
2 c. sliced okra
1 c. water
Salt and pepper to taste
⅛ t. cayenne pepper
⅓ t. thyme
1 t. chopped parsley
1 6-oz. can crabmeat
1 lb. fresh shrimp, cleaned and cooked

Melt butter in skillet. Sauté onion, green pepper, celery, ham and garlic until onion is transparent. Add tomatoes, okra, water and seasonings. Simmer 15 minutes. Add crab and shrimp. Cook 10 minutes or until okra is tender. Serve over steaming rice. Serves 6 to 8.

NEW ENGLAND CLAM CHOWDER

¼ c. diced bacon
½ c. minced onion
1 10¼-oz. can frozen cream of potato soup
¼ c. milk
2 6-oz. cans minced clams
1 T. lemon juice
⅛ t. pepper

In large saucepan, cook and stir the bacon and onion until the bacon is crisp, and onion is tender. Stir in soup and milk. Heat through, stirring occasionally. Stir in clams and liquor, lemon juice and pepper. Heat through. Serve with saltines. Serves 4.

CHICKEN GUMBO SOUP

1½ qt. chicken stock
½ c. chopped onion
¼ c. finely chopped green pepper
1 c. tomatoes, fresh or canned
½ t. baking soda
1 c. chopped okra, fresh or canned
½ c. or more cooked rice

If using fresh okra, cook for 20 minutes. In a large pot, sauté onion in 2 T. butter until golden brown. Add green pepper, tomatoes, baking soda and okra and cook for 5 minutes. Add chicken stock; simmer for 20 minutes. Add rice 5 minutes before end of cooking time. Serve hot. Serves 6 to 8.

SOUTHERN GUMBO

¼ c. bacon drippings or butter
1 large onion, chopped
2 c. canned tomatoes
1½ t. salt
½ t. pepper
3 c. okra, sliced
3 c. bouillon
1 c. uncooked rice

Melt drippings or butter in large heavy soup kettle. Add onion. Sauté until lightly browned. Add remaining ingredients. Tightly cover. Heat to boiling, then reduce heat. Simmer for 30 minutes. Serve hot. Serves 6.

CLAM CHOWDER

2 6-oz. cans minced clams
2 slices bacon, diced
½ c. minced onions
2 T. finely chopped celery
2½ c. raw potato, cut in ½-inch cubes
½ c. hot water
¼ c. domestic Sauterne wine
1½ c. milk
2 T. butter
2 t. salt
¼ t. pepper
⅛ t. cayenne pepper

Drain clams, reserving liquid. Sauté bacon, onion and celery until onion is golden. Add clam liquid, diced potatoes, water and wine. Cover. Cook for 20 minutes or until potatoes are tender but still firm. Add clams, milk, butter, salt, pepper and cayenne pepper. Bring to a boil, stirring occasionally. Serve hot. Serves 6.

SEAFOOD MUSHROOM CHOWDER

¼ c. chopped onion
¼ c. chopped green pepper
2 T. oil
1 10½-oz. can chicken broth
1¼ c. water
1 4-oz. can mushrooms
1 t. salt
1 lb. fish, cut in 1-inch cubes
1 10-oz. pkg. frozen peas and carrots, thawed
1 8-oz. can white potatoes, drained and cubed
1 c. cooked shrimp
2 T. cornstarch
½ c. light cream

In a large soup kettle, sauté onion and green pepper in oil until soft. Add water, mushrooms, chicken broth, salt, fish and vegetables. Bring to a boil. Cover and simmer for 10 minutes. Add shrimp. Combine cornstarch and cream and stir into chowder. Heat over low heat, stirring constantly until chowder thickens. Serves 4 to 6.

CAPE COD CHOWDER

2 lbs. cod fillets, cut in 2-inch pieces
¼ c. butter or margarine
1 lb. small white onions, halved
1 qt. boiling water
1 lb. potatoes, peeled and thinly sliced
2 carrots, peeled and sliced
2 T. Worcestershire sauce
1 t. salt
1 bay leaf
2 c. milk
1 c. heavy cream

Melt butter in heavy skillet. Add onions and sauté until golden. Cover and simmer for 10 minutes. Add water, potatoes, carrots, Worcestershire sauce, salt and bay leaf. Bring to a boil. Reduce heat and simmer, covered, for 10 minutes. Lay fish on top. Cover and simmer for 20 more minutes or until vegetables are tender and fish flakes easily. Scald milk; stir in cream. Gradually add fish mixture. Heat only until hot; do not boil. Serve with crispy crackers. Makes 3 quarts.

YANKEE PARSNIP CHOWDER

¼ lb. lean salt pork, cubed
4 medium parsnips, peeled and cubed
1 stalk celery, diced
1 large potato, peeled and diced
1 large onion, peeled and chopped
1 qt. water
Salt to taste
⅛ t. pepper
½ c. milk
Nutmeg
2 T. minced parsley

In a large heavy soup kettle, lightly brown salt pork. Pour off most of the drippings. Add parsnip, potato, celery and onion. Stir fry over moderate heat until glazed, about 5 minutes. Add water, salt, if needed, and pepper. Cover. Simmer 2 hours. Uncover and simmer, stirring occasionally for an additional 45 minutes. Add milk. Simmer for 15 minutes longer. Ladle into soup bowls. Top with grated nutmeg and sprinkle with parsley. Serve hot.

CORN CLAM COD CHOWDER

1 lb. frozen cod
½ c. chopped onion
2 T. butter or margarine
2 c. frozen sliced potatoes
1 6½-oz. can minced clams
1 t. salt
⅛ t. pepper
1 c. corn
1 c. evaporated milk
1 T. chopped dill

Simmer fish in water to cover until fish flakes easily with a fork. Drain and set aside. Sauté onion in butter until golden. Add potatoes, 2 cups water and liquid from clams. Cover and simmer 5 minutes or until potatoes are tender. Add salt, pepper, corn, clams and cooked fish broken up in pieces. Add milk. Heat to a boil. Ladle into soup bowls and sprinkle with dill. Serves 6.

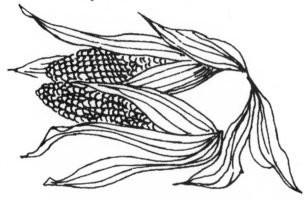

OLD-FASHIONED CORN CHOWDER

1 c. cubed bacon
1 medium onion, diced
4 T. flour
2 c. cubed raw potatoes
2 c. corn, fresh, canned or frozen
2 c. water
2 c. milk
1 t. salt
½ t. pepper

Sauté bacon until crisp. Remove from pan. Fry onions in bacon fat until soft. Stir in flour. Add milk slowly, stirring until thick. Cook potatoes and corn in water until potatoes are tender. Add onion gravy to potato mixture. Add bacon and seasoning. Serve hot. Stir over flame until well mixed and mixture boils. Serves 6 to 8.

CRABMEAT AND CORN CHOWDER

2½ c. corn
1 c. crabmeat, cooked and flaked
1 T. minced onion
2½ c. scalded milk
2½ c. thin cream sauce
2 egg yolks
Salt and pepper
Dash of nutmeg
1 T. butter

Put corn, onion, and hot milk in top of double boiler. Cook over boiling water 20 to 25 minutes. Cool slightly. Puree in blender until smooth. Add Thin Cream Sauce to corn mixture. Beat egg yolks. Add a little of hot mixture to the egg yolks, then add to chowder. Season to taste. Add nutmeg. Just before serving add crabmeat and butter. Serves 8.

THIN CREAM SAUCE

2 T. butter
2 T. flour
2½ c. milk

Melt butter over low heat. Add flour, blending with butter. Stir in milk and simmer until sauce thickens slightly.

PRAIRIE CORN AND BEEF CHOWDER

¼ lb. salt pork, diced
1 3-oz. pkg. dried beef
2 medium onions, peeled and minced
1 medium potato, peeled and diced
¼ c. green pepper, minced
½ t. paprika
¼ t. basil
⅛ t. pepper
2 c. cream-style corn
4 c. milk
½ t. salt

Brown salt pork in large heavy skillet over moderate heat. Remove from pan. Frizzle chipped beef 1 to 2 minutes. Remove from pan. Add onions, potato, and green pepper to pan. Sauté for 10 minutes. Add seasonings, corn, milk, pork and chipped beef. Over low heat, simmer for 20 minutes. Add salt to taste and serve. Serves 6.

Chilled Soup

SWEDISH FRUIT SOUP

¾ c. raw rice
½ c. currants
½ lb. seedless raisins
1 c. sugar
8 c. boiling water
½ lb. prunes
  Juice of 1 lemon
  Rind of 1 lemon, chopped
4 apples, diced, not peeled

Soak dried fruits 1 hour in warm water. Mix with rest of ingredients and stew for 1 hour. Delicious served either hot or cold. Serves 4 to 6.

VICHYSSOISE

1 c. diced raw potatoes
¼ c. sliced green onions
1 c. raw peas
½ c. diced celery
1½ c. chicken broth
  Salt and pepper to taste
1 c. heavy cream
¼ c. chopped chives for garnish

Place potatoes, onions, peas, celery and chicken broth in kettle. Bring to a boil. Simmer for 20 minutes or until vegetables are tender. Cool. Blend in cream. Serve icy cold topped with chopped chives. Can be served hot. Serves 4.

COLD CUCUMBER SOUP WITH CHICKEN

1 cucumber, peeled, seeded and diced
½ c. sweet cider
½ c. sour cream
½ c. heavy cream
1 c. chopped cooked chicken
½ t. salt
  Dash pepper
  Chopped chives

Puree cucumber with cider in blender. Add to sour cream, heavy cream and chicken. Season to taste. Chill. Serve in chilled soup cups and garnish with chives. Makes 3 cups.

GAZPACHO

1 10¾-oz. can tomato soup
1 soup can water
1½ c. mixed vegetable juice
1 T. lemon juice
1 t. seasoned salt
¼ c. sliced, pitted ripe olives
1 c. croutons
1 c. shredded raw carrots
1 c. diced avocado
1 c. sliced green onions

Blend tomato soup, water, vegetable juice, lemon juice and seasoned salt in a large bowl. Chill for several hours, as soup tastes best when frosty cold. Stir in ripe olive slices. Place bowl in a bowl of crushed ice to keep cold. Ladle soup into serving cups. Top with shredded carrots, croutons, avocado or green onions. Serves 6.

CHERRY SOUP

4 c. fresh cherries, pitted
8 c. water
4 lemon or orange slices
1 c. sugar
1 dumpling recipe
  (see Soup Accompaniments)

Add pitted cherries and other ingredients to a saucepan. Bring to a boil and boil until cherries are soft. Drop small dumplings into mixture and cover. Simmer gently 10 minutes to cook dumplings. Set aside to cool. Chill in refrigerator and serve ice cold. Serves 6.

CHILLED AVOCADO SOUP

1 large avocado, peeled and pitted
½ c. half and half cream
1½ c. chicken broth
   Salt to taste
   Sour cream for garnish
   Paprika

Blend avocado until smooth. Add cream and chicken broth. Blend a few seconds. Add salt. Pour into soup dishes, garnish with a spoonful of sour cream and sprinkle lightly with paprika. Serves 6.

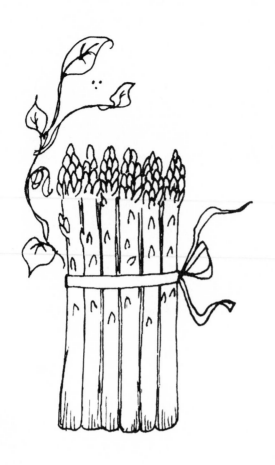

SWISS CHERRY SOUP

½ c. seedless raisins
¼ c. lemon juice
1 2-inch stick cinnamon
6 slices naval orange
5 thin slices lemon
3 c. water
2 c. pitted dark sweet cherries,
fresh or frozen
2 c. sliced fresh peaches, peeled
½ c. honey
Salt to taste
2 T. cornstarch
¼ c. cold water
Yogurt for garnish

Combine raisins, lemon juice, cinnamon stick, orange and lemon slices. Add to water in a saucepan. Bring to a boil over medium heat. Reduce heat. Cover and simmer for 15 minutes. Remove cinnamon stick. Add cherries, peaches, honey and salt to soup mixture. Bring to a boil. Blend cornstarch and cold water. Stir into soup. Bring to a boil, stirring until soup is clear, about 2 or 3 minutes. Remove from heat. Pour into a covered bowl and cool for several hours. Serve with yogurt. Serves 4 to 6.

CHILLED CREAM OF ASPARAGUS SOUP

½ c. water
2 c. thinly sliced asparagus
1 c. white sauce
1½ c. milk
¼ c. sour cream
½ t. salt
⅛ t. pepper

Bring water to a boil in a saucepan. Add asparagus and simmer for 5 minutes. In electric blender combine white sauce, milk, sour cream, salt and pepper, cooking liquid and asparagus. Whirl at high speed for 2 minutes or until smooth. Refrigerate, covered, overnight. Serve chilled with a dollop of sour cream added to each bowl. Serves 4.

WHITE SAUCE

1 T. butter or margarine
1 T. flour
1 c. milk

Melt butter; stir in flour. Gradually add milk, stirring until blended and thickened.

ICE COLD TOMATO SOUP

2 7½-oz. cans tomato sauce
2 T. chopped green onion
1½ t. salt
1 t. instant powdered chicken broth
¼ t. celery salt
⅛ t. pepper
1 c. dry white wine
½ c. water
1 T. fresh dill weed or ¾ T. dried dill weed
Sprigs dill for garnish
Thin cucumber slice for garnish

In blender, place tomato sauce, onion, salt, instant powdered chicken broth, celery salt and pepper. Cover and puree for 30 seconds or until smooth. Add wine, water and dill weed. Blend for 10 seconds. Refrigerate for 1½ hours or until chilled. Just before serving whirl in the blender for a few seconds. Pour into bowls. Garnish with fresh dill and cucumber slice. Makes 4 servings.

CHILLED CUCUMBER SOUP

1½ c. sliced, peeled cucumber
1 c. chicken broth
2 T. onion, finely chopped
2 T. yogurt
1 t. fresh dill or ¼ t. dried dill weed
   Salt and pepper to taste
1 cucumber, thinly sliced for garnish

Combine cucumber, broth and onion in saucepan. Heat to boiling. Reduce heat and cook until cucumbers are translucent, about 10 minutes. Cool slightly. Pour into blender and puree until smooth. Chill for 1½ hours in refrigerator. Before serving, stir in yogurt, dill weed and seasoning. Garnish with additional cucumber slices. Makes 2 servings of 1 cup each.

BUTTERMILK SOUP

4 c. buttermilk
3 T. honey
3 eggs
   Juice of 1 lemon

In blender, puree ingredients until smooth. In saucepan, heat until boiling. Simmer 10 minutes. Cool. Chill in refrigerator. Serve with a very thin slice of cucumber floating on top of the bowl. Serves 6.

BOUILLON ON THE ROCKS

2 or 3 ice cubes
1 10¼-oz. can bouillon
   Twist of lemon or sprig of mint

Pour undiluted bouillon over ice cubes. Garnish with twist of lemon or sprig of mint. Serves 3.

AEBLESUPPE
DANISH APPLE SOUP

5 medium apples, unpeeled and quartered
½ t. grated lemon peel
2 T. cornstarch
¼ c. cold water
½ c. white wine
½ c. sugar
1 t. cinnamon

Simmer apples and grated lemon rind in water for 15 minutes. Strain. Dissolve cornstarch in the cold water. Add to the apple mixture, stirring constantly until clear. Add wine, sugar and cinnamon. Simmer for 5 minutes. Serve hot or cold. Serves 4.

CHILLED ROSE-HIP SOUP

4 c. ripe rose-hips, bruised with a
   rolling pin
   Water
1 c. sugar
2 T. cornstarch

Cover rose-hips with water in a saucepan. Bring to a boil and boil for 10 minutes. Strain through a cheesecloth. Discard hips and return liquid to heat. Add enough water to make 4 cups. Add sugar, bring to boil. Turn off heat. Mix cornstarch with ¼ cup water. Stir into soup. Return pan to heat and cook until soup is clear and lightly thickened. Cool soup and chill. Serve with a dab of whipped cream on each portion. Serves 4.

CUCUMBER FRAPPÉ

2 c. pared, cubed cucumber
2 T. minced parsley
1 green onion, trimmed and sliced
¼ c. instant nonfat dry milk
1 c. cold water
1 t. lemon juice
1 t. salt
⅛ t. hot seasoning, optional
   Parsley for garnish

Combine cucumber, parsley, green onion, instant milk, water, lemon juice and seasoning in electric blender. Whirl until foamy and smooth. Pour into small juice glasses. Garnish with sprig of parsley. Makes 6 servings.

PARADISE SOUP

- 5 c. tomato juice
- 1 c. sour cream
- ¼ c. grated onion
- 2 T. lemon juice
- 1 t. grated lemon rind
- Salt and white pepper to taste
- ¾ c. diced cooked ham
- 1 cucumber, cut in balls
- 1 cantaloupe, cut in balls
- ¼ c. fresh basil, minced

In a large bowl whisk the tomato juice, sour cream, onion, lemon juice, lemon rind and seasonings. Stir in ham. Chill the soup, covered, for 4 hours. Cut ball of cucumber and cantaloupe and sprinkle with basil. Chill for 4 hours. Pour soup into chilled bowls. Garnish each serving with cucumber and melon balls. Serves 4 to 6.

GUACAMOLE CREAM SOUP

1 large avocado, peeled and pitted
1 slice onion
1 c. heavy cream
1 t. instant chicken base
½ t. salt
3 drops red pepper seasoning, optional
2 c. milk

Slice avocado into blender container. Add onion and ½ cup of the cream. Cover. Whirl until smooth. Beat in remaining cream, instant chicken base, seasoning and milk. Chill. Pour into chilled cups or mugs. Sprinkle with paprika. Serves 4 to 6.

MOCK VICHYSSOISE

¼ c. wild leeks or wild onions, white part only
4 c. strong chicken broth
2 c. boiled Jerusalem artichokes, peeled and sliced
1 c. light cream
Salt and pepper to taste
Chives, finely cut for garnish

Simmer leeks in chicken broth 15 minutes or until tender. Add Jerusalem artichokes and place in blender. Blend until smooth. Return to saucepan. Add cream and seasonings. Reheat to simmering. Serve hot or cold. Garnish with chives. Serves 6.

CHILLED CHICKEN SOUP

1 c. cooked chicken, finely chopped
3½ c. chicken broth
½ t. curry powder
4 egg yolks, well beaten
2 c. light cream
Salt

Combine chicken broth, chicken and curry powder in soup kettle. Bring to a boil. Add a little hot broth to beaten egg yolks. Blend with cream. Slowly stir into hot soup. Stir until slightly thickened. Chill. Serve with chopped chives sprinkled on each serving. Serves 6 to 8.

BUTTERMILK SHRIMP SOUP

4 c. buttermilk
1 8-oz. pkg. frozen cooked shrimp
1½ cucumber, peeled and chopped
½ c. green pepper, seeded and chopped
6 radishes, sliced
1 t. salt
¼ t. pepper
1 T. fresh chopped dill

Combine all ingredients except dill. Cover and refrigerate at least 12 hours. Add dill before serving. Serves 6.

MADRILENE

2 12-oz. cans Madrilene
Sour cream for garnish
Minced chives for garnish
Red caviar for garnish
Freshly ground black pepper

Chill 2 cans of Madrilene for 4 hours or until set. Turn out into a bowl and break up with a fork. Spoon into chilled bouillon cups or bowls. Top each portion with a dollop of sour cream, finely chopped chives and freshly ground black pepper. Center a small spoonful of red caviar in each mound of sour cream. Serve at once. Serves 4 to 6.

BUTTERMILK SOUP II

2 c. buttermilk
2 c. mixed vegetable juice
1 T. sugar
½ t. salt
½ t. onion powder
Watercress or dill for garnish

Combine buttermilk, vegetable juice, sugar, salt and onion powder. Beat well. Chill. Serve in glasses or cups. Garnish with watercress or dill sprigs. Serves 4.

Cream Soup

CREAM OF BROCCOLI SOUP

8 c. water
3 cubes chicken bouillon
2 10-oz. pkgs. frozen broccoli, chopped
2 T. onion flakes
1 t. salt
½ t. pepper
¾ c. powdered milk
1 T. sherry

In a saucepan, combine water and bouillon cubes. Bring to a boil. Add frozen broccoli, onion flakes and seasonings. Bring to a boil, then reduce heat. Simmer for 15 minutes or until broccoli is tender. Cool slightly. Put a third of the broccoli mixture into blender with ¼ cup of the powdered milk. Blend until smooth. Pour into clean pan. Repeat until all broccoli and powdered milk is blended. Just before serving, heat, stirring in sherry. Serves 6 to 8.

CREAM OF PEA SOUP

1 12-oz. pkg. frozen peas
2 c. water
Milk or cream
¼ c. butter
¼ c. flour
1 small onion, chopped
1 t. salt
¼ c. chopped ham for garnish

Put peas and onion in 2 cups of water in a saucepan. Cook for 15 minutes or until soft. Cool slightly. Puree vegetables and water in blender. Measure, adding enough milk or cream to make 4 cups. Set aside. Melt butter in a saucepan. Add flour and mix well. Gradually add the pea mixture to the flour mixture. Simmer, stirring all the time. Add salt. Garnish with chopped ham. Serves 4 to 6.

CREAM OF SPINACH SOUP

4 c. frozen spinach, thawed
½ c. boiling water
½ c. butter
½ c. finely chopped onion
½ c. flour
½ gal. milk
2 t. salt
Grated Provolone cheese

Cook spinach in water, simmering until tender. Drain. Run through a sieve or cool slightly and puree in blender. Melt butter. Sauté onion until tender but not brown. Blend in flour. Gradually stir in milk and cook until smooth. Add spinach and salt. Heat to boiling; simmer until thickened. Serve with a sprinkling of cheese on each bowl. Makes 2 quarts soup.

CREAM OF CARROT SOUP

¼ c. butter
5 medium carrots, finely chopped
1 onion, finely chopped
1 t. salt
4 c. chicken stock
½ c. rice
1 c. light cream

Melt butter in a large saucepan. Add carrots, onion and salt. Cover. Simmer for 15 minutes, stirring constantly. Add chicken stock and rice. Simmer, covered, for 45 minutes or until carrots are very tender. Strain through a fine sieve or blend in a blender. Reheat, adding cream and serve. Makes 1½ quarts soup.

CREAM OF ASPARAGUS SOUP

1½ c. cooked asparagus
1 small onion, chopped
2 c. asparagus water
2 T. butter, melted
2 T. flour
1 c. whole milk
Salt and pepper to taste

Hold out a few cooked asparagus tips for garnish. Rub the rest through a sieve or puree in a blender. Cook onion in asparagus water until tender. Add pureed asparagus. Add butter and flour that have been blended together. Stir well. Add milk. Heat over medium heat until slightly thickened. Season to taste. Serve hot, topped with asparagus tips. Serves 4.

CREAM OF PIMIENTO SOUP

2 c. hot milk
2 c. chicken broth
4 T. butter
2 T. flour
2 T. cold milk
1 c. pimiento
1 t. grated onion
½ t. salt
Dash cayenne pepper

Place hot milk and chicken broth in top of double boiler. Heat. Cream together the butter, flour and cold milk. Add to mixture in double boiler. Boil, stirring constantly until thickened. Run pimientos through a sieve. Add to soup. Add onion and seasonings. Mix well and serve hot. Serves 6.

CREAM OF GREEN ONION SOUP

2 T. butter or margarine
2 c. thinly sliced green onions
¼ t. salt
2 T. flour
2 c. boiling water
1⅔ c. evaporated milk
Grated cheese

Melt butter in soup kettle. Add onions and salt. Cover. Cook slowly until onions are tender, or about 5 minutes. Remove from heat. Sprinkle with flour, stirring to blend. Add water and boil until slightly thickened, stirring constantly. When ready to serve, add milk and reheat. Sprinkle each serving with grated cheese, if desired. Serves 4.

CHEESE SOUP

2½ c. raw celery, diced
2 c. water
¼ c. butter
2 T. flour
1½ t. salt
2 c. American cheese, cubed, about ½ lb.
½ c. light cream

In blender combine 1 cup of the water with celery. Blend at high speed until celery is liquified. Pour into saucepan. Combine in blender the remaining 1 cup water and rest of ingredients. Blend at high speed until smooth. Add to celery mixture in saucepan. Simmer over low heat for 15 minutes, stirring constantly. Add more water if thinner soup is desired. Serves 8.

CREAM OF ONION SOUP

3 c. sliced onions
1 cup sliced celery
¼ c. butter
1 t. salt
1 t. paprika
½ t. ground ginger
¼ t. cloves
¼ t. cinnamon
¼ t. pepper
3½ c. chicken stock
¼ c. raw rice
2 c. milk
¼ c. cream
Grated lemon rind of 1 lemon

In a large soup kettle, sauté onion and celery in butter for 5 minutes. Add spices. Add chicken stock and bring to a boil. Add rice. Simmer for 30 minutes or until rice and vegetables are done. Cool slightly. Puree soup in blender. Pour back into soup kettle. Add milk. Simmer for 5 minutes. Add cream and grated lemon rind. Serve at once. Serves 4.

CREAM OF CHICKEN SOUP

1 5-lb. stewing chicken, cut up
10 cups water
¼ c. chopped celery
¼ c. chopped onion
1 bay leaf
1 T. salt
¼ c. parsley, chopped
Butter
Flour

Place chicken and other ingredients in a large soup kettle. Simmer for 3 hours or until chicken is tender. Remove meat from chicken. Measure stock and return to kettle. Add chicken meat. Measure butter and flour, using 1 tablespoon for each cup of stock. Melt butter in a saucepan. Add flour. Mix. Add stock a little at a time, stirring constantly. Cook 5 minutes after it comes to a boil. Serve with crispy crackers. Serves 6 to 8.

CREAM OF CELERY SOUP

4 c. celery and leaves, cut small
2 t. salt
4 c. water
½ c. butter
½ c. flour
Milk or cream
½ c. shredded American cheese for garnish

Combine celery and leaves, water and salt. Simmer for 1 hour, or until tender. Cool slightly. Puree in blender, adding enough milk or cream to make 4 cups. Melt butter in saucepan; stir in flour. Pour in celery-milk mixture slowly. Bring to a boil, stirring constantly. Serves 4 to 6.

CHEDDAR CHEESE SOUP

½ c. mild cheddar cheese, diced
1 T. flour
¼ c. chicken stock
¼ c. cream
1¼ c. milk
1 T. butter
1 small clove garlic
1 egg yolk

Combine butter, garlic and 1 cup of the milk in a saucepan. Heat, melting butter, and set aside. In top of double boiler, combine cheese, flour and remaining ¼ cup milk. Heat until cheese melts. Add chicken stock and simmer for 15 minutes. Stir in butter mixture, discarding garlic. Just before serving, stir in egg yolk that has been mixed with cream. Garnish with grated Parmesan cheese. Serves 4.

CREAM OF LETTUCE SOUP

4 c. chopped lettuce
2 T. minced onion
2½ c. water
½ t. salt
2 T. vegetable oil
2 T. flour
2 T. wheat germ
2½ c. hot milk
⅛ t. pepper

Add minced onion and lettuce to boiling, salted water. Lower heat. Simmer for 20 minutes. In double boiler, cream oil and flour with wheat germ. Stir in hot milk. Cook for 30 minutes. Add lettuce mixture and heat. Serves 6.

CREAM OF TOMATO SOUP

3½ c. canned tomatoes
1 small onion stuck with 3 cloves
1 bay leaf
1 T. parsley, chopped
¼ t. baking soda
1 6-oz. can tomato paste
¼ c. butter
¼ c. flour
2 c. milk
1½ t. salt
1 T. sugar

Simmer tomatoes, onion, bay leaf and parsley in large saucepan for 10 minutes. Cool slightly. Puree in a blender. Add soda and tomato paste. Mix well. Melt butter in saucepan. Blend in flour. Add milk. Cook until thick and smooth, stirring constantly. Add salt. Add tomato mixture, a little at a time. Blend well. Add sugar. Bring to a simmer. Serve at once. Serves 4 to 6.

CREAM OF VEGETABLE SOUP

2 c. cooked vegetables, pureed or chopped
1 c. meat or vegetable stock
1 to 2 T. minced onion
1 to 2 T. butter or margarine
2½ c. milk
2 T. quick-cooking tapioca
Salt and pepper
2 T. minced parsley

For vegetables use spinach, green beans, peas, asparagus, corn, potatoes, carrots, celery or lima beans or a combination of many of them. Chop or puree vegetables. Set aside. Melt butter and sauté onion in top of double boiler for 2 minutes. Add milk, stock and quick-cooking tapioca. Bring to a boil, stirring constantly. Place over boiling water; add vegetables and reheat. Season. Sprinkle with minced parsley. Serve hot. Serves 6.

26

Pictured opposite
Cream of Vegetable

Foreign Soup

MULLIGATAWNY SOUP

3 medium carrots, pared and sliced
2 stalks celery, sliced
3 c. diced, cooked chicken
6 c. chicken stock
1 large onion, chopped
¼ c. butter or margarine
1 apple, pared, cored and chopped
5 t. curry powder
1 t. salt
¼ c. flour
1 T. lemon juice
2 c. hot cooked rice
¼ c. chopped parsley
6 lemon slices

Cook carrots and celery in 1 cup chicken stock for 20 minutes or until tender. Add chicken. Heat until hot. Cover and keep warm. In Dutch oven sauté onion in butter until soft. Add apple, curry powder and salt. Sauté for 5 minutes or until apple is soft. Add flour. Gradually add remaining chicken stock, stirring constantly. Reduce heat and cover. Simmer 15 minutes. Add carrots, celery, chicken and their stock. Bring to a boil. Stir in lemon juice. Serve with rice, chopped parsley and lemon slices. Serves 6.

EGG SOUP

4 c. bread crumbs
½ c. butter
1 egg
2 c. water
2 c. milk
Salt to taste

Melt butter in heavy skillet. Add bread crumbs. Brown, stirring to coat with butter. Break egg over the bread and stir until mixed and cooked. Pour bread into a tureen. Pour water and milk into skillet, salting well. Bring to a boil, then pour over bread. Eat at once.

EAST INDIAN STYLE BLACKEYE BEAN SOUP

1 c. blackeye beans
1 onion, chopped
2 T. coconut
¼ t. turmeric
1 t. honey
¼ t. cumin
3 c. water

Add all ingredients to boiling water. Simmer until beans are done, 1½ to 2 hours. More water may be needed as water is absorbed in cooking. Salt to taste. Serves 4.

BONE MEAL SOUP (CALDO DE HUESO)

2 lbs. beef bones
8 c. water
2 onions, chopped
2 carrots, scraped and diced
Salt to taste
2 c. rice
4 bananas
1 c. chopped cabbage

In large soup kettle, combine beef bones, water, onions, carrots and salt. Stew for 2 hours. Add rice, bananas and cabbage. Cook for 30 minutes. Serve with crusty homemade bread. Serves 4 to 6.

FINNISH SUMMER SOUP KESAKEITTO

2½ c. water
1 T. sugar
¼ t. salt
2½ c. milk
1 10-oz pkg. frozen peas
½ head cauliflower, cut into flowerets
1 medium carrot, diced
5 small potatoes, peeled and quartered
1 egg yolk
2 T. butter or margarine
1 T. chopped chervil or parsley

In a large saucepan place water, sugar and salt. Bring to a boil. Add milk, peas, cauliflower, carrot and potatoes. Simmer for 10 to 15 minutes, or until vegetables are tender. Stir in a tablespoon of hot soup to beaten egg yolk. Add to soup. Season to taste. Add margarine and herbs. Serve immediately. Serves 6 to 8.

ARMENIAN MEATBALL SOUP

½ lb. lean ground beef
½ c. fine cracked wheat or bulgur
1 egg
1 T. flour
2 T. tomato sauce
1 t. salt
4 c. water
4 c. chicken or beef broth
1 medium onion, peeled and minced
¼ c. uncooked long-grain rice
1 c. canned chick-peas, rinsed and loose
  skins discarded
2 T. butter or margarine
1 T. dried, crushed mint leaves
3 T. lemon juice

Combine meat, wheat, egg, flour, tomato sauce and ½ t. salt. Shape into small meatballs, using a scant tablespoon of mixture for each ball. Bring water and ½ t. salt to a boil. Drop in 6 or 7 meatballs. When boiling, reduce heat and simmer for 10 minutes. Remove with slotted spoon. Cook the rest of the meatballs and set aside. Discard water and rinse out pot. Add broth to pot and bring to a boil. Add onion and rice. Simmer for 20 minutes. Add meatballs and chick-peas. Add melted butter, lemon juice and mint. Simmer 1 minute. Serves 6.

ROMAN EGG SOUP
WITH NOODLES
(STRACCIATELLA CON PASTA)

4 c. chicken broth
1 c. cooked noodles
4 eggs
1½ T. semolina or flour
1½ T. grated Parmesan cheese
⅛ t. salt
⅛ t. pepper
1 T. chopped parsley

Place chicken broth in large soup kettle. Bring to a boil. Add cooked noodles to broth and boil. Beat eggs in a bowl until thick. Combine with flour, cheese, salt and pepper. Stir a little broth into eggs. Slowly pour the egg mixture into boiling broth, stirring constantly. Continuing to stir, simmer for 5 minutes. Top with parsley. Serves 4. *Note:* To cook noodles, heat 3 cups water and 1 teaspoon salt to boiling. Add one cup noodles. Simmer until tender. Drain.

HUNGARIAN GOULASH

2 T. oil
4 lbs. beef stew meat, cut in ½-inch pieces
2 c. chopped onions
¼ c. flour
4 c. beef broth
2 c. peeled, seeded, chopped tomatoes *or*
  1 8-oz. can tomatoes
½ c. dry red wine
¼ c. parsley
2 T. paprika
1½ t. marjoram
1½ t. thyme
1 t. salt
½ t. caraway seed
  Grated peel of 1 lemon
⅛ t. pepper
¾ c. sour cream

Heat oil in Dutch oven. Add meat and brown on all sides. Add onion. Sauté until tender. Stir in flour until smooth. Add beef broth, tomatoes and remaining ingredients, except sour cream. Simmer for 2 to 3 hours, covered, until meat is tender. Stir occasionally. Serve with sour cream and spaetzle. Serves 8.

GERMAN OXTAIL SOUP
(OCHSENSCHWANZSUPPE)

2 oxtails, well trimmed
2 medium onions, cut in wedges
1 large carrot, quartered
2 c. celery and tops, cut in 3-inch pieces
1 T. salt
¼ t. pepper
4 cloves
8 c. water
1 carrot, peeled and diced
1 parsnip, or small turnip, peeled
  and diced
2 slices boiled ham, diced
2 c. fine noodles

Place oxtails, onions, carrot, celery, salt, pepper and cloves in large soup kettle. Add water. Cover. Bring to a boil. Reduce heat. Simmer for 4 hours or until meat loosens from bones. Strain. Discard vegetables. Remove meat from bones. Dice. Measure liquid. Add water to make 8 cups. Bring to a boil. Add diced carrots and parsnip. Boil 10 minutes. Add meat, ham and noodles. Cook until noodles are just tender. Serve hot. Serves 6 to 8.

29

FEATHER FOWLIE

1 2½-lb. chicken, whole
1 12-oz. slice smoked ham
2 onions, chopped
2 stalks celery, chopped
1 carrot, scraped and sliced
4 T. finely chopped parsley
¼ t. thyme
⅛ t. nutmeg
1 t. salt
  Dash of pepper
3 egg yolks
½ c. heavy cream

Place chicken in a heavy kettle. Add ham, onions, celery, carrot, parsley, water and seasonings. Bring to a boil. Reduce heat. Simmer, covered, for 1 hour. Cool slightly. Remove meat from bones. Cut chicken and ham in small pieces. Put chicken bones in kettle. Simmer for an additional hour. Strain broth and chill in the refrigerator for 4 hours. Skim fat from the top of the broth. Reheat broth; add chicken and ham. Beat together eggs and cream. Add to hot soup, stirring to mix well. Heat but do not boil. Garnish with parsley. Serves 8.

BASQUE FISH SOUP

1 large onion, chopped
½ c. chopped celery
1 clove garlic, crushed
2 16-oz. cans tomatoes
½ c. dry white wine
½ c. minced parsley
1 t. salt
¼ t. pepper
¼ t. thyme
1 lb. frozen cod fillets, cut in
  1-inch chunks
4 c. fish stock or water

In a large soup kettle sauté onion, celery and garlic in butter until tender. Stir in tomatoes, wine, parsley, salt, pepper and thyme. Cover and simmer for 30 minutes. Add fish and simmer 7 to 10 minutes or until fish is opaque and flakes easily with a fork. Makes 4 to 6 servings. Good served with crusty bread and a salad of mixed greens.

COCK-A-LEEKIE

1 1½-lb. chicken, whole
6 c. water
2 T. butter
6 leeks, sliced or 2 c. chopped scallions
1 t. salt
2 T. finely chopped parsley

Place chicken in stewing pot deep enough so chicken is covered with water. Simmer for 1 hour or until chicken is tender. Cool. Cut meat into thin strips. Thoroughly chill chicken broth. Skim off fat that forms on top. Melt butter in skillet. Add leeks, salt and pepper. Cover. Simmer over low heat for 15 minutes or until leeks are soft and tender. Add to chicken broth and chicken. Simmer another 10 minutes. Garnish with parsley.

CHINESE EGG DROP SOUP

4 c. chicken broth
2 eggs, lightly beaten
2 T. parsley, chopped

Bring chicken broth to a boil. Keeping broth in motion, slowly pour the beaten egg into the hot broth so that it cooks in threads. Serve immediately. Sprinkle parsley on top of each serving. Serves 4 to 6.

CREAM OF CARROT
AND RICE SOUP
(CREME DE CRECY)

5 c. strong chicken broth
2 c. coarsely chopped carrots
3 T. raw rice
½ c. light cream
  Salt to taste
½ t. chili powder
½ t. lemon juice
  Avocado for garnish

In large soup kettle, combine broth, carrots and rice. Simmer until carrots and rice are tender. Cool slightly. Puree in a blender. Heat cream. Add to mixture in blender. Add salt, chili powder and lemon juice. Blend again. Pour into soup bowls. Garnish with bite-sized slices of avocado. Serves 4 to 6.

LIVER DUMPLING SOUP
(LEBERKNOEDELSUPPE)

¼ lb. beef liver
1 egg
2 T. melted margarine or butter
¾ c. fine bread crumbs
1 small onion, finely chopped
1 t. parsley flakes
¼ t. dried marjoram
¼ t. salt
4 c. beef bouillon

Remove membrane from liver. Mince finely or chop in blender. Combine liver, egg, margarine, bread crumbs, onion, parsley, marjoram and salt. Mix well. Chill about 25 minutes. Bring bouillon to a boil. Form meat mixture into 4 dumplings. Drop dumplings into simmering bouillon. Cook 10 minutes. Serve dumplings with bouillon in large soup bowls. Serves 4.

BASQUE SHRIMP SOUP

1 large onion, chopped
½ c. chopped celery with leaves
1 clove garlic, crushed
2 T. butter
2 16-oz. cans tomatoes
½ c. white wine
½ c. minced parsley
1 t. salt
¼ t. pepper
¼ t. thyme
1 12-oz. pkg. frozen raw shrimp

In a large saucepan, sauté onion, celery and garlic in butter until tender. Stir in tomatoes, wine, parsley, salt, pepper and thyme. Cover and simmer for 30 minutes. Add shrimp and simmer 7 to 10 minutes. Remove from heat. Let stand 1 minute. Serve at once.

DUTCH PRETZEL SOUP

3 T. butter
2 T. flour
4 c. milk
2 c. water
   Salt and pepper to taste
2 lbs. pretzels, broken into small pieces
1 t. parsley, chopped

In large pot, melt butter; stir in flour. Gradually stir in milk mixed with the water. Simmer and stir until thickened. Add salt and pepper. Just before serving, add pretzels and sprinkle with parsley. Serves 6.

TEARS OF SNOW SOUP

8 c. chicken broth
2 stalks celery, diced
¼ lb. fresh mushrooms, diced
1 2½-oz. can water chestnuts, drained, rinsed and diced
1 t. soy sauce
   Salt and pepper
2 scallions, minced

Heat chicken broth to boiling. Add remaining ingredients except scallions. Simmer 5 minutes. Garnish with Egg Threads and scallions. Serves 6.

EGG THREADS

2 eggs
2 T. sherry
   Dash of salt

Beat eggs lightly with the sherry and salt. Grease skillet with oil and heat. Pour the egg mixture slowly into skillet, tipping pan from side to side so that the mixture spreads thinly and evenly. Cook over low heat until egg is set and edges curl away from pan. Invert on a plate. Cool. Cut in narrow strips 2 inches long and ⅛ inch wide.

SHRIMP BISQUE
(POTAGE BISQUE DE CREVETTES)

1 lb. cleaned shrimp
3 T. butter
1 carrot, sliced
2 scallions or leeks, sliced (white part of leek)
¼ c. brown rice, uncooked
½ bay leaf
1 t. dried thyme
3 sprigs parsley
   Salt and pepper to taste
   Dash of cayenne pepper
   Dash of paprika
2 ripe tomatoes, chopped
8 c. water
1 c. dry white wine, optional
¾ c. cream, half and half

Sauté carrot, scallions and shrimp in butter in large soup kettle. Add remaining ingredients except cream. Simmer, uncovered, for 40 minutes. Remove bay leaf and parsley. Cool slightly. Whirl in blender in small batches, then return to soup kettle. Add cream. Reheat slowly. Serves 10 to 12.

BASQUE TUNA SOUP

1 large onion, chopped
½ c. chopped celery
1 clove garlic, crushed
2 T. butter
2 16-oz. cans tomatoes
½ c. dry white wine
½ c. minced parsley
1 t. salt
¼ t. pepper
¼ t. thyme
2 7-oz. cans tuna, drained

Sauté onion, celery and garlic in butter until tender. Stir in tomatoes, wine, parsley, salt, pepper and thyme. Cover and simmer for 30 minutes. Add tuna fish to boiling tomato mixture. Heat and serve. Serves 4 to 6.

HAWAIIAN AVOCADO SOUP

3 ripe avocados, peeled, seeded and cubed
3 c. chicken broth
1 t. lemon juice
1 clove garlic, minced
  Dash of salt and pepper
1½ c. light cream
½ c. heavy cream, whipped
½ c. macadamia nuts, coarsely chopped

In an electric blender, combine avocado, chicken broth, lemon juice, garlic and seasoning. Puree until creamy. Pour into a large bowl. Add light cream. Stir until well mixed. Chill thoroughly. When ready to serve, ladle into small bowls. Top with a spoonful of whipped cream and sprinkle with macadamia nuts. Serves 6.

NORTHERN SALMON SOUP
(NORRLANDSK LAXSOPPA)

3 T. barley
2 medium carrots, peeled and diced
1 medium turnip, peeled and diced
1 medium onion, chopped
1 16-oz. can pink salmon
1 t. salt
  Dash pepper
2 T. chopped parsley

Add water to salmon liquid to make 5 cups. Add barley and boil 30 minutes. Add vegetables and cook for 10 to 15 minutes or until tender. Add salmon pieces and seasoning. Heat thoroughly. Top with parsley. Serve hot. Serves 4.

NORWEGIAN PEA SOUP
WITH PORK

1 1-lb. pkg. green or yellow split peas
8 c. boiling water
¼ lb. salt pork
1 large carrot, pared and diced
1 large stalk celery plus leaves, diced
5 green onions plus tops, sliced
  Salt to taste
¼ t. pepper

Sort peas. Place in large heavy soup kettle. Add boiling water and salt pork. Cover and simmer over moderate heat for 1½ hours. Add carrot, celery, green onions, salt and pepper. Simmer covered for 30 minutes. Uncover and simmer for 1 to 1½ hour stirring occasionally until quite thick. Ladle into soup bowls and serve. Serves 6.

ROMAN EGG SOUP

4 c. chicken broth
4 eggs
1½ T. semolina *or* flour
1½ T. grated Parmesan cheese
⅛ t. salt
⅛ t. pepper
1 T. chopped parsley

Bring chicken broth to a boil. Beat eggs until thick. Combine with flour, cheese, salt and pepper. Slowly pour egg mixture into boiling broth, stirring constantly. Simmer, stirring constantly for 5 minutes. Top with parsley. Serves 4.

VENETIAN RICE AND PEA SOUP
(RISI E BISI)

3 T. chopped onion
6 T. butter or margarine
1 10-oz. pkg. frozen peas
½ t. salt
3 13¾-oz. cans chicken broth
1 c. rice
3 T. chopped parsley
⅔ c. freshly grated Parmesan cheese

In large saucepan or Dutch oven, sauté onion in butter until golden. Add peas and salt and cook for 2 minutes, stirring often. Add broth. Bring to a boil. Add rice, stirring thoroughly. Simmer for an additional 25 minutes or until rice is tender. Add parsley. Remove from heat. Add Parmesan cheese just before serving. Serves 6.

Hearty Soup

BEEF SHANK SUPPER SOUP

  4 lbs. meaty beef shanks,
    cut 1½ inch thick
  1 large onion, finely chopped
  2 stalks celery, finely chopped
  1 1¾-lb. can whole tomatoes
  1 t. thyme
  ¼ t. cloves
  1 T. oregano
  1 bay leaf
1½ t. salt
  6 c. water
  ½ c. pearl barley
  4 large carrots, cut in 1-inch chunks
  1 10-oz. pkg. frozen cut beans
  1 c. chopped parsley

In large soup kettle, brown meat in its own fat over medium heat. Remove and set aside. Add onion and celery to drippings in kettle. Sauté until onion is tender. Add tomatoes. Stir in seasonings and water. Add meat and bring to a boil. Reduce heat. Simmer covered for 1½ hours. Remove meat from broth. Refrigerate broth and skim fat from top. Trim meat, discarding fat and connective tissue. Return meat and bones with marrow to kettle. Heat to simmer. Add barley, carrots and beans. Cook, uncovered, for 50 minutes or until beans are tender. Add parsley and salt to taste. Serves 6.

TURKEY CHILI

  1 medium onion, chopped
  ½ c. chopped green pepper
  2 T. vegetable oil
  2 c. cooked and diced turkey
  1 20-oz. can red kidney beans
  2 c. canned or fresh tomatoes, chopped
  2 t. chili powder
  2 c. water or beef broth
    Salt and pepper to taste
    Cooked rice

Sauté onion and green pepper in oil until tender. Stir in remaining ingredients, except rice. Heat to boiling. Reduce heat and simmer for 15 minutes stirring occasionally. Serve over rice. Serves 6.

MINER'S SPICED KETTLE OF BEEF AND VEGETABLES

  2 lbs. boneless beef chuck, cut in 1-in. cubes
  ½ c. flour
  1 T. salt
  ½ t. pepper
  ½ t. paprika
  2 T. shortening or vegetable oil
  1 c. chopped onion
  6 c. water
    Garni (1 clove and 1 t. pickling spice in cloth)
  3 c. peeled and chopped fresh tomatoes or
    3 c. drained, canned tomatoes
  2 c. diced carrots
  1 c. sliced celery
  3 c. diced potatoes
  1 c. green peas
  1 t. sugar
  2 t. salt
  ¼ t. pepper
  3 T. cornstarch blended with ¼ c. cold water

Dredge beef cubes in mixture of flour, salt, pepper and paprika. Brown in fat on all sides in large heavy kettle. Add onion and brown lightly. Add water and garni. Simmer, covered for 30 minutes. Add vegetables and seasonings. Simmer, uncovered, for 30 minutes or until done. Blend some of the hot gravy into the cornstarch mixture and stir into stew until thick. Serves 8 to 10.

TURKEY NOODLE SOUP

  2 turkey drumsticks
  8 c. stock or water
  1 large onion, chopped
  2 stalks celery with leaves, chopped
  1 carrot, diced
  2 T. minced parsley
  1 t. salt
  ⅛ t. pepper
  1 recipe homemade noodles or
    2 c. prepared noodles

Place turkey drumsticks in stock with seasonings. Bring to a boil. Reduce heat. Simmer for 1½ hours or until meat falls from bone. Remove bones. Cut meat in small pieces and return to stock. Add vegetables and simmer for 30 minutes. Add noodles and simmer 20 minutes more. Add parsley before serving. Serves 6.

Pictured opposite
Miner's Spiced Kettle of Beef and Vegetabl

CHICKEN AND NOODLE SOUP

1 3 to 3½-lb. broiler cut up
4 c. water (or more)
1 onion, diced
1 stalk celery, diced
1 t. salt
½ t. pepper
   Homemade noodles

Place broiler in stewing kettle. Add water to cover. Add onion, celery, salt and pepper. Bring to boil; skim off froth. Turn down heat and simmer for 1 hour or until well done. Strain broth from chicken. Allow chicken to cool and take meat from bones. Put broth back in kettle. Bring to boil. Drop in noodles, stirring so that they separate. Simmer for 20 minutes. Add meat from chicken. Heat.

HOMEMADE NOODLES

2 eggs
1 t. salt
3 T. water
2 c. flour

Beat eggs, water and salt. Mix in flour until it is a stiff dough. Place on floured board. Roll out with rolling pin into large oval. Roll up like jelly roll after flouring top to keep from sticking. Slice with knife into narrow strips. Unroll and add to broth.

OXTAIL SOUP

4 lbs. oxtails
½ c. flour
1 t. salt
2 T. shortening
6 c. hot water
3 medium potatoes, diced
1 medium turnip, cubed
4 carrots, diced
½ c. celery, sliced
1 medium onion, chopped

Coat oxtails with mixture of flour and salt. Brown on all sides in heavy kettle, in melted shortening. Add water. Heat to boiling. Reduce heat and simmer 3½ hours, covered. Add vegetables. Simmer for 30 minutes or until vegetables are tender. Add more water if necessary. Just before serving, may be thickened slightly by mixing 3 tablespoons flour in ¼ cup water. Add to the broth. Serve hot with crispy crackers. Serves 6 to 8.

BEEF NOODLE SOUP

3 lbs. beef neck bones or short ribs
1 large onion, diced
6 c. water, more as needed
2 stalks celery, diced
1 t. salt
1 pkg. medium-wide noodles or homemade noodles

Cook bones or short ribs in salted water with onion and celery until meat is tender. Remove bones. Return meat to stock. Add noodles and cook until tender, about 30 minutes. Serve hot. Serves 4 to 6.

CHICKEN SOUP WITH RICE

8 c. chicken stock
½ c. carrots, cut small
1 c. celery stalks, chopped
1 small onion, diced
2 c. cooked chicken, chopped
1 t. salt
⅛ t. pepper
½ c. brown or white rice
2 T. parsley flakes

Put cold chicken stock and vegetables in large soup kettle. Bring to boil. Reduce heat and simmer until vegetables are about half done. Add rice and cook until done. Add chicken. Heat to boiling. Add parsley. Pour into soup dishes while piping hot. Serve with crispy crackers. Serves 6.

CHILI CON CARNE

2 T. butter
1 clove garlic
½ c. chopped onion
1 lb. ground beef
½ t. salt
1 T. flour
1 large can kidney beans
1 T. chili powder
1 large can tomatoes

Melt butter in large heavy kettle. Add garlic and onion. Cook until soft. Add meat. Sprinkle with salt and flour. Stir and cook until meat is browned. Add other ingredients. Cover. Simmer 1 hour or more. Serve in bowls with crackers. Serve hot. Serves 4 to 6.

BEEF MUSHROOM SOUP WITH GREENS

1 lb. beef chuck, cut in ½-in. cubes
2 T. oil
2 c. sliced mushrooms
1 large onion, chopped
6 cups water
1 28-oz. can tomatoes
1 t. salt
⅛ t. pepper
1 bay leaf
⅓ c. brown rice
4 c. torn fresh spinach, escarole, or other greens

In a large, heavy kettle or Dutch oven, lightly brown meat in oil. Add mushrooms and onions and sauté until tender. Add water, tomatoes and seasonings. Simmer for 1 hour. Stir in rice. Cover and simmer for 45 minutes or until rice is tender. Add spinach. Cover and simmer for 10 minutes or until tender. Discard bay leaf. Makes 8 servings.

BEEF BARLEY SOUP

3 lbs. beef neck bones or short ribs
1 large onion, chopped
1½ c. barley
6 c. water
2 stalks celery, diced
1 t. salt

Cook neck bones or short ribs in salted water with onion and celery for about 2 hours or until meat is tender. Add water as needed. Remove meat from bones. Return meat to stock. Add barley and cook for 45 minutes more or until barley is done. Serve hot. Serves 4 to 6.

BROCCOLI AND CHICKEN SOUP

1 bunch broccoli, chopped and cooked
1½ c. boiling water
2 10½-oz. cans chicken soup
1 c. milk
Salt and pepper to taste
Croutons
Grated Parmesan cheese

Blend broccoli in blender until smooth. Combine broccoli puree, soup, milk, salt and pepper to taste. Heat. Top with croutons and Parmesan cheese. Serves 4.

VEGETABLE BEEF SOUP

3 lbs. meaty soup bones, beef neck bones
1½ lbs. soup meat, cubed
3½ qts. cold water
1 t. salt
1 c. celery, diced
3 medium onions, chopped
6 celery stalks, diced
6 carrots, diced
3 medium potatoes, diced
1 large can tomatoes

Place soup bones and soup meat in large soup kettle. Add water and salt. Simmer, covered, for 3 to 4 hours or until meat is tender. Remove bones. Take any meat there is from bones. Strain broth. Return meat to broth. Skim off excess fat with a spoon. Add vegetables and simmer 30 to 45 minutes. Serves 6 to 8.

VENISON SOUP

1 lb. venison, cut in cubes
1 c. diced turnips
½ c. minced parsley
1 c. minced onion
2 c. diced celery
6 c. venison stock *or* beef stock
3 bay leaves
½ t. thyme
1 c. tomato paste
3 t. sugar
Salt and pepper to taste

Combine all ingredients in a large soup kettle. Simmer over low heat for 2 hours. Serves 6 to 8.

BOLOGNA SOUP

1 ring bologna, chopped
½ c. chopped celery
½ c. chopped carrots
1 onion, chopped
2 medium potatoes, diced
1 c. chopped cabbage
2 green peppers, chopped
1 c. canned tomatoes *or* fresh tomatoes, peeled and chopped
4 c. water

Cook bologna in water for 30 minutes. Add vegetables. Cook for an additional 30 minutes. Serves 6.

THREE BEAN CHILI

1 lb. dry soybeans
1 c. dry pinto beans
1 c. dry chick-peas
2 T. vegetable oil
2 large onions, chopped
2 large green peppers, chopped
2 16-oz. cans tomatoes
2 envelopes instant beef broth *or*
2 cubes beef bouillon
1 T. cumin
2 T. chili powder
1 t. salt
¼ t. pepper

Wash and drain beans and chick-peas. Cover with water and bring to a boil. Reduce heat. Cover and simmer for 2½ hours. Sauté onions and green pepper in oil until tender, stirring often. Add to bean mixture with remaining ingredients. Simmer for 1 more hour. If thicker chili is desired cook uncovered for the last hour. Serves 12.

GOULASH SOUP

2 T. butter
1½ c. finely chopped onion
2 c. cubed red and green sweet peppers
2 t. finely chopped garlic
1 T. caraway seeds
2 T. paprika
2 T. soy sauce
2 T. whole wheat flour
1½ c. cubed potatoes
1 c. thinly sliced cabbage
1 1-lb. can tomatoes
4 c. water
1 lb. beef bones
2½ c. leftover beef, cut into ¾-inch pieces

Melt butter in a large saucepan. Add onions and peppers. Sauté until tender but not soft. Add minced caraway and garlic to onions and pepper. Sprinkle with paprika. Stir in soy sauce and flour. Simmer for 5 minutes, stirring constantly. Add potatoes, cabbage, tomatoes, water, meat and bones. Simmer 45 minutes. Remove bones and serve. Serves 8 to 10.

WHITE BEAN, PARSNIP POTATO AND TURNIP SOUP

1 1½-lb. soup bone
1 c. dried navy or pea beans, washed and sorted
2 c. boiling water
3 medium potatoes, thinly sliced
2 medium white turnips, thinly sliced
1 large parsnip, thinly sliced
2 t. salt
¼ t. pepper
1½ c. fine, stale, but not dry, bread crumbs
1 medium onion, peeled and thinly sliced for garnish

Boil soup bone in water to cover for 2 hours or until meat falls off bone. Discard bones after removing all meat. While the soup bone boils, soak beans in boiling water in a small saucepan. Add beans and the soaking water to soup kettle. Cover and simmer for 1 hour. Add vegetables and salt and pepper. Cover and simmer an additional 1½ hours. Uncover and simmer ½ hour longer. Stir in bread crumbs. Top each portion with a slice or two of onion. Serves 8.

FRONTIER LAMB OR BEEF AND DUMPLINGS

2 lbs. boned lean lamb shoulder or beef chuck, cut in 1-inch cubes
4 t. bacon drippings or shortening
2 large onions, peeled and chopped
½ t. sage
½ t. thyme
¼ t. pepper
2 t. chili powder
2 t. salt
2 large tomatoes, peeled, cored and chopped
4 c. beef stock or water
1 recipe for dumplings (see Soup Accompaniments)

Brown lamb or beef on all sides in bacon drippings in a large heavy kettle. Drain on paper towel. Add onions to kettle and sauté in remaining drippings for 10 minutes or until lightly browned and tender. Add meat to kettle. Add seasonings, tomatoes, juice and beef stock or water. Cover and simmer slowly 1½ to 2 hours until meat is tender. Drop dumplings into stew and steam for 10 minutes. Serves 6.

Light and Diet Soup

CAULIFLOWER SOUP

2 c. cauliflower, sliced
4 c. chicken broth
1 c. chopped green onions
1 t. salt

Heat chicken broth. Add cauliflower, green onions and salt. Simmer until vegetables are tender. Serves 4.

MUSHROOM BROTH

6 T. butter
¾ lb. white mushrooms, thinly sliced
¼ c. minced scallions
2 T. lemon juice
6 c. beef broth, hot
3 T. Madeira

In a heavy saucepan melt butter. Add mushrooms, scallions and lemon juice. Cover and steam over low heat for 8 to 10 minutes, or until tender. Add hot broth and Madeira. Bring to a boil and simmer for 10 minutes. Serve in heated soup cups. Serves 6.

MUSHROOM SOUP

½ lb. mushrooms, chopped
2 T. chopped onion
2 T. vegetable oil
2 c. beef or chicken stock
1 t. salt
2 T. flour
2 c. cream

Brown onion and mushrooms in oil. Put stock in soup kettle. Add mushrooms, onions, salt and flour mixed with a bit of cold water. Stir to blend. Heat to boiling. Add cream and heat, but do not boil. Serve hot. Serves 4.

ORIENTAL CUCUMBER SOUP

8 c. chicken broth
2 T. soy sauce
1 t. sugar
1 T. sherry
½ lb. pork, cut in long thin strips
2 medium cucumbers
Salt and pepper to taste

In a large saucepan, combine broth, soy sauce, sugar, sherry and pork strips. Bring to a boil. Reduce heat and simmer for 10 minutes. Peel cucumbers and cut in half, lengthwise. Scoop out seeds. Slice and add to soup. Simmer until cucumber becomes transparent. Serves 8.

SQUASH SOUP

3 c. uncooked squash
3 c. milk
½ c. dry skim milk powder
1 T. minced parsley
2 c. water
1 T. flour
1 T. vegetable oil
2 T. brown sugar
1 t. salt

Cook squash in salted water until soft. Cool slightly. Drain. Rub through sieve or mash. Combine other ingredients with squash in a soup kettle. Bring to a boil. Simmer for 10 minutes. Sprinkle with extra parsley on top of bowls. Serves 4.

OLD-FASHIONED TOMATO SOUP

2 c. tomatoes fresh or canned
½ t. baking soda
2 c. milk
1 T. butter
1 t. salt
½ t. pepper

Place tomatoes in a large saucepan. If using fresh tomatoes, simmer until tender. If canned, bring to a boil. Add soda. In another pan, scald milk. Add milk to tomatoes and stir. Add butter, salt and pepper, stirring well. Serve immediately with crisp crackers. Serves 4. *Note:* The soda prevents the acid of the tomatoes from curdling the milk.

SPINACH SOUP

4 c. meat stock or milk
2 T. vegetable oil
1 t. salt
1 T. flour
1 onion, finely chopped
2 lbs. fresh spinach, washed and stemmed
3 slices bacon, diced and fried crisp for garnish

In an electric blender, chop all ingredients, except bacon, blending only a little of the spinach at a time. Put blended mixture into a soup kettle. Cover. Bring to a boil. Reduce heat and simmer for 10 minutes. Garnish individual servings with bacon. Serves 4.

CREAMY ONION SOUP

3 large onions, thinly sliced
2 shallots, chopped
¼ c. butter
1 t. salt
¼ t. pepper
4 c. water
2 egg yolks
½ t. lemon juice

Melt butter in a large skillet and sauté onion and shallots over moderate heat until tender. Add salt and pepper. Cook covered over low heat for 45 minutes, stirring occasionally. Stir in cold water. Bring to a boil and simmer for 10 minutes. Beat egg yolks, lemon juice and a little of the hot soup. Stir into soup mixture. Cook over low heat for 2 or 3 minutes or until it is slightly thickened; but do not boil. Serves 4.

CORN SOUP

2 c. fresh, frozen or canned corn
4 c. milk
2 T. vegetable oil
2 T. flour
Salt and pepper

Combine corn and milk in soup kettle. Bring to a boil; simmer gently for 20 minutes. Cream oil and flour and slowly blend into corn-milk mixture until smooth. Season with salt and pepper to taste. Serves 4.

DANDELION BROTH

2 c. very young dandelion leaves
6 c. water
½ c. finely chopped chives
Salt to taste
Lemon peel twists

Drop dandelion leaves in boiling water to cover and boil for 1 minute. Drain. Bring 6 cups water to a boil. Add chives and blanched dandelion leaves. Simmer, covered, for 15 minutes. Strain. Salt to taste. Serve hot with twist of lemon peel. Serves 8.

VIOLET GREENS SOUP

2 c. heart-shaped violet leaves, stems removed, packed
1 c. watercress with stems removed, packed
4 T. butter or margarine
4 wild leeks, white parts only, finely chopped
2½ c. water
4 T. cornstarch
2 c. heavy cream
Salt and pepper to taste

Rinse and drain violet leaves and watercress. Chop leaves. Melt butter in skillet and sauté greens and leeks for 15 minutes. Remove from heat. Add 2 cups water. Mix cornstarch with ½ cup water. Stir into greens. Return to heat and cook until thickened, stirring constantly. Gradually add cream and warm. Add salt and pepper. Pour into warm soup tureen. Garnish with violet flowers just before serving. Serves 6.

ORIENTAL BEEF BROTH

2 10½-oz. cans condensed beef broth
2 c. water
1 c. uncooked fine noodles
½ c. dry sherry
2 T. thinly sliced green onions
2 t. soy sauce

In a medium saucepan, mix beef broth, water and noodles. Bring to a boil. Reduce heat. Cover and simmer for 10 minutes. Remove from heat. Add sherry, green onions and soy sauce. Makes 6 servings.

A BROTH OF GREENS

6 c. water
1 c. chopped mustard leaves (packed down)
1 c. chopped dock leaves (packed down)
1 clove garlic, crushed
2 slices bacon, diced
  Salt to taste
½ c. Pernod or anise liqueur

Bring water to a boil. Add mustard, dock, garlic, bacon and salt. Turn heat low and simmer, covered, for 30 minutes. Strain out solids and put aside to serve. Add Pernod or liqueur to broth. Serve hot with toast. Serves 6 to 8.

DRIED CORN SOUP

1 lb. lean boned beef chuck, cut in 1-in. cubes
1 T. bacon drippings or butter
4 c. water
1 c. dried corn *or* 2 c. fresh corn
½ t. salt
⅛ t. pepper

Over high heat, brown meat on all sides in fat. Add water. Cover and simmer for 1 hour. Add dried corn, salt and pepper. Cover and simmer 1 hour or until both meat and corn are tender. Serves 4.

FRENCH ONION SOUP

3 c. thinly sliced onion
2 T. butter or margarine
6 c. beef consommé
½ t. salt
⅛ t. pepper
6 slices French bread
  Grated cheese

Melt butter in a heavy 3-quart saucepan. Sauté onion slowly, turning frequently, until golden. Add consommé, salt and pepper. Simmer about 15 minutes. Under broiler, toast one side of French bread slices. Spread untoasted side with butter. Cut each slice in half and sprinkle with cheese. Broil until cheese melts. Float slices of toast, sprinkled with additional cheese, on each dish of soup. Serves 6.

WATERCRESS SOUP

1 large bunch watercress
1 bunch parsley
2 green onions and tops
2 or 3 new potatoes
4 c. water
  Salt and pepper to taste
1 c. light cream

Clean and coarsely chop watercress, parsley and green onions. Peel potatoes and quarter. Combine all vegetables in saucepan and cover with water. Cook until potatoes are tender. Cool slightly. Blend for a few seconds in a blender. Return to saucepan. Add light cream, if desired. Heat, but do not boil. Serves 4 to 6.

WATERCRESS SOUP II

¼ lb. lean pork
8 c. chicken broth
1 onion, chopped
1 t. sherry
1 celery stalk, thinly sliced
1 t. salt
  Dash of pepper
1 to 1½ c. watercress, stems removed and chopped

Cut pork in thin shreds. Heat chicken broth in large soup kettle. Add pork. Simmer 10 minutes. Add remaining ingredients, except watercress. Simmer 10 more minutes. Add watercress. Simmer 2 minutes. Serve at once. Serves 6 to 8.

SPROUT SOUP

1 c. bean sprouts
2 c. water
2 chicken bouillon cubes
2 t. soy sauce
½ t. salt
¼ t. pepper

Use either canned bean sprouts or other sprouts that you have grown. Drain. Add to water in which bouillon cubes have been dissolved. Heat to boiling. Add soy sauce and seasonings. Serves 2.

GREEK LEMON SOUP

- 2 10¾-oz. cans condensed chicken broth
- 2 cans water
- ⅓ c. raw rice
- 4 eggs
- 2 T. lemon juice
- ½ t. salt
- Parsley for garnish

Combine chicken broth and 2 cans water. Bring to a boil. Add rice and cover. Simmer for 20 minutes or until rice is tender. Set aside. Beat eggs until frothy. Slowly beat in lemon juice and 1 cup of the hot broth mixture. Stir egg mixture into soup. Heat slowly, stirring occasionally. Sprinkle with parsley. Serves 6 to 8.

ALMOND SOUP

- 1 c. chopped onion
- 3 T. butter
- 8 c. chicken broth
- ½ c. raw rice
- 1 t. salt
- ½ t. pepper
- ½ t. saffron
- 1 c. finely ground blanched almonds
- 3 hard-cooked egg yolks, finely chopped
- 3 T. minced parsley

Sauté onion in butter until golden. Add broth and bring to a boil. Cover and simmer for 10 minutes. Stir in rice, salt, pepper and saffron. Simmer 20 more minutes. Stir in almonds and simmer for 10 minutes. Add egg yolks and parsley. Serves 10 to 12.

Stew and Ragout

VENISON AND VEGETABLE SOUP

1½ lbs. venison, cubed
 2 T. vegetable oil
 ½ c. flour
 1 t. salt
 8 c. water
 2 onions, chopped
 4 carrots, cut in chunks
 4 potatoes, cut in chunks
 2 parsnips, cut in chunks
 2 turnips, cut in chunks
 1 10½-oz. can tomato soup
 2 T. Worcestershire sauce
 2 T. flour
 ¼ c. water

Coat venison with flour and brown in oil in heavy soup kettle. Drain off excess fat. Add water and salt. Simmer for 2 hours or until meat is tender. Add vegetables and more water if needed. Add Worcestershire sauce and tomato soup. Simmer for an additional 45 minutes or until vegetables are tender. Blend flour and water. Stir into hot stew, stirring until thickened. Simmer for 10 minutes. Serve hot. Serves 6 to 8.

IRISH STEW

 6 medium potatoes, quartered
 1 lb. lamb neck or shoulder slices, fat removed
 2 medium onions, sliced
    Salt and pepper to taste
 ¼ t. thyme
 1 bay leaf
 1 small head cabbage, cut in thin wedges

In a heavy saucepan, arrange alternate layers of vegetables and meat with just enough water to cover. Add seasonings. Bring to a boil, cover and simmer over low heat for 2 to 2½ hours or until all is tender. Shake pan now and then to prevent sticking. Serves 4.

BEEF RAGOUT

 1 8-oz. pkg. brown and serve sausages, cut in 1-in. pieces
 2 lbs. lean beef, cut in 1½-inch cubes
 ¼ c. flour
 1 t. salt
 ¼ t. pepper
 2 T. vegetable oil
 2 c. chopped leeks, white part only
 4 stalks celery, cut in 2-inch pieces
 2 c. rutabaga, cubed
 1 clove garlic, minced
 1 1-lb. can tomatoes
 1 10¾-oz. can condensed beef broth
    Water
 1 t. Italian mixed herbs, crumbled
 ½ c. chopped parsley

Brown sausages in heavy kettle or Dutch oven. Remove with slotted spoon. Combine beef cubes, flour, salt and pepper in a plastic bag. Shake until meat is evenly coated. Brown beef, a few pieces at a time, in pan drippings or add vegetable oil. Remove with slotted spoon. Brown leek, celery and rutabaga and remove with slotted spoon. Set aside. Return sausage, beef, flour in bag to kettle. Add tomatoes, beef broth plus water to make 3½ cups liquid and herbs. Cover and simmer 1½ hours. Add vegetables and simmer until done. Can be frozen. Serves 8.

WINTER SQUASH SOUP

 1 medium winter squash, peeled and chopped
 ½ medium onion, chopped
 1 handful celery leaves, chopped
 1 medium tomato, chopped
 8 c. water or more
    Salt and pepper to taste
 2 T. brown sugar
 1 t. cinnamon
    Drippings from steak and onions for seasoning

Cover squash with water in large soup kettle. Add chopped onion, celery leaves, and tomato. Bring to a boil. Reduce heat and simmer until squash is tender. Season with salt and pepper to taste. Add brown sugar and cinnamon. Serve with drippings from steak and onions to season. Serves 4.

ITALIAN LAMB STEW

2 lbs. lamb neck slices
2 T. vegetable oil
1 small onion, sliced
1 clove garlic, minced
1 20-oz. can tomatoes
1½ t. salt
¼ t. oregano leaves
⅛ t. pepper
1 bay leaf
2 medium zucchini, diced
¼ lb. small mushrooms
2 20-oz. cans white kidney beans
½ c. stuffed olives

Brown lamb in oil. Remove lamb. Discard drippings. Combine onion, garlic, tomatoes, salt, oregano, pepper and bay leaf in the skillet. Add lamb and cover. Simmer for 45 minutes then remove the bay leaf. Add zucchini and mushrooms. Cook for 15 minutes or until vegetables and lamb are tender. Drain kidney beans and add to lamb mixture. Add olives and cook 5 minutes longer. Serves 6.

RABBIT STEW

1 3½-lb. rabbit, dressed
1 c. wine vinegar
1 c. red table wine
1 c. sliced onion
2 bay leaves
3 t. salt
½ t. cloves
¼ t. thyme
¾ t. hot sauce, optional
1 c. flour
½ c. shortening
1 c. water or stock
2 t. sugar

Cut rabbit in serving-size pieces. Combine vinegar, wine, onion, bay leaves, 2 t. salt, cloves, thyme and hot sauce. Mix well. Add rabbit and marinate in refrigerator for 2 days. Drain rabbit. Strain and reserve marinade. Combine flour and 1 teaspoon salt. Coat rabbit. Brown in shortening. Drain off excess fat. Add marinade and water. Cover and simmer for about 45 minutes or until tender, stirring occasionally. Add sugar. Serves 3 to 4.

INJUN STEW

4 lbs. game, cut in serving size pieces
6 slices bacon, diced
4 medium onions, sliced
8 c. tomatoes
4 potatoes, cubed
  Salt and pepper to taste
2 c. corn
2 c. lima beans

In a Dutch oven, brown the game and bacon. Add onions near the end of the browning. Add the liquid from the tomatoes and enough water to cover the game in the kettle. Add salt, pepper, potatoes and tomatoes. Cover and simmer until tender. Add corn and beans just before serving. Serve with a hot chunk of corn bread. *Note:* Squirrel, rabbit, old cock pheasant or grouse are all good for this hunters dish.

PIONEER STEW
WITH PARSLEY DUMPLINGS

1½ lbs. beef chuck neck bones
4 t. vegetable oil
3 medium onions, chopped
1 clove garlic, peeled and crushed
½ c. diced green pepper
½ t. sage
½ t. thyme
¼ t. pepper
2 t. salt
1 t. chili powder
2 large tomatoes, peeled and chopped
1 qt. water
2 small acorn squash, halved, seeded and cut in ¾ inch cubes
  Parsley dumplings (see Soup Accompaniments)

Brown beef bones in oil in heavy kettle. Remove. Add onions, garlic and green pepper. Sauté until golden. Add seasonings. Return beef bones to kettle. Add tomatoes and water and simmer for 2 hours. Take meat off bones; add meat and squash to soup and simmer for 10 minutes. Drop dumplings by rounded teaspoonfuls to bubbling soup. Reduce heat and simmer, uncovered, 10 minutes. Cover and simmer for 10 more minutes to fluff up dumplings. Spoon a dumpling or two into each bowl and top with stew. Serves 6.

HUNTERS MULLIGAN

4 lbs. shank or bony part of large
    game animal
2 t. salt
1 t. pepper
1 large can tomatoes or 1 qt. home-
    canned tomatoes
1 can peas
3 slices bacon, diced
4 medium potatoes, quartered
3 medium onions, quartered
3 medium carrots, cut in chunks
2 T. flour
¼ c. cold water

Place shanks or other bony, but meaty, pieces, salt and pepper in large soup kettle. Cover with cold water. Simmer until meat is tender. Add tomatoes, peas, bacon, potatoes, carrots and onions. Simmer until vegetables are done. If broth is too thin, mix flour and water together and stir into soup. Cook 10 minutes longer. Serve with hot baking powder biscuits. Serves 6 to 8.

OLD-FASHIONED LAMB STEW

2 lbs. lamb stew meat, cubed
2 T. vegetable oil
3 carrots, cut in chunks
3 potatoes, cut in chunks
2 large onions, quartered
3 stalks celery, cut in 1-inch slices
8 c. water
1 t. salt
⅛ t. pepper
2 T. Worcestershire sauce
2 T. flour
¼ c. water
2 T. parsley

In a large heavy soup kettle, brown meat in oil. Add water and salt. Bring to a boil. Reduce heat and simmer for 1 hour. Add vegetables and seasonings. Simmer for an additional hour or until meat and vegetables are tender. Blend together flour and water. Stir into meat mixture and cook until thickened. Add parsley. Serves 4 to 6.

CHICKEN STEW
WITH CARROT DUMPLINGS

1 stewing chicken, cut up
1 medium onion, sliced
1 stalk celery, sliced
2 t. salt
⅛ t. thyme
⅛ t. pepper
3 T. flour
⅓ c. water
    Carrot dumplings (see Soup
    Accompaniments)

Put chicken, onion, celery, seasonings and water to cover in a large kettle or Dutch oven. Bring to a boil. Cover. Reduce heat and simmer for 2½ to 3 hours or until chicken is tender. With slotted spoon remove chicken. Cool enough to remove bones from meat. Skim fat from broth. Blend in flour mixed with water and stir over medium heat until slightly thickened. Add chicken meat. Bring to a boil. Drop in dumplings. Cover and simmer for 15 minutes. Serves 8.

ZUCCHINI AND PEPPER STEW

1 6-oz. can tomato paste
1 c. water
1 carrot, sliced
1 stalk celery, sliced
½ c. vegetable oil
2 medium zucchini, diced
4 large green peppers, seeded and diced
4 small potatoes, diced
1 large onion, chopped
1 clove garlic, minced
    Salt and pepper to taste
    Grated Italian cheese

Combine tomato paste, water, carrot and celery in saucepan. Bring to a boil. Reduce heat and simmer for about 1 hour or until celery is tender. In skillet, sauté zucchini, green pepper, potatoes, onions, and garlic. Stir frequently until lightly browned. Add to tomato mixture. Season with salt and pepper. Cover and simmer 10 minutes or until vegetables are tender. Serve with cheese. Serves 4.

MEATBALL AND VEGETABLE STEW

1 lb. ground chuck
1 c. fine dry bread crumbs
1 T. grated cheese
2 eggs
½ c. water
1 t. salt
⅛ t. pepper
⅓ c. vegetable oil
1 large onion, sliced
1 clove garlic, minced
2 bay leaves
1 8-oz. can tomato sauce
2 stalks celery, diced
¼ t. mixed herbs
2 carrots, peeled and sliced
3 large potatoes, peeled and diced
1 7-oz. pkg. frozen Italian style
    green beans

Lightly mix the first seven ingredients and shape into 16 balls. Brown meatballs on all sides in oil. Remove meatballs. Sauté onion and garlic until golden. Add bay leaves and tomato sauce. Cook 5 minutes. Add 1½ cup water, celery and herbs. Simmer for 15 minutes. Add meatballs, carrots, potatoes and green beans. Simmer, covered, for 45 minutes or until vegetables are tender. Serves 4 to 6.

BRUNSWICK STEW

2 3-lb. broilers
1 lb. salt pork, chopped
2 qts. freshly cut corn
5 qts. sliced peeled tomatoes
1 qt. diced potatoes
2 qts. lima beans
2 medium onions, chopped
¼ t. ground red pepper, optional
    Salt and pepper to taste

Cut up chicken. Cover with water in a heavy soup kettle. Cook until meat falls off the bones, adding water if necessary. Add salt pork, vegetables and seasonings. Simmer slowly until tender and mixture is thick. Serve hot. Makes 15 to 20 servings. Recipe can be cut in half.

VEAL AND MUSHROOM STEW

1½ lbs. veal, cut in cubes
    Vegetable oil
½ t. basil
1 clove garlic, minced
1 t. onion powder
¼ t. thyme
1 large can mushrooms with liquid
1 10¾-oz. can beef consommé
1 8-oz. can tomato sauce
3 carrots, diced
3 potatoes, diced
3 onions, chopped
    Flour

Brown veal in small amount of oil. Add basil, garlic, onion powder, thyme, mushrooms, beef consommé and tomato sauce. Bring to a boil. Simmer for 2 hours. Add vegetables. Simmer for 30 minutes longer. Thicken with a small amount of flour mixed with water, if desired. Serves 4 to 6.

SQUIRREL BRUNSWICK STEW

10 squirrels, dressed and disjointed
 4 c. whole kernel corn
½ lb. salt pork, diced
 5 lbs. potatoes, diced
 8 c. canned tomatoes
 3 lbs. onions, diced
 2 lb. lima beans
 1 c. diced celery
    Salt and pepper to taste
¼ c. Worcestershire sauce
    Flour

Place squirrels in large kettle with enough water to half cover. Bring to a boil. Cover and simmer until the squirrels are tender. Cool. Remove squirrels from stock. Remove meat from bones. Add meat and remaining ingredients except flour. Cook for 2 hours. Thicken with small amount of flour mixed with water. Simmer for 30 minutes longer. Serves 20.

PORK RAGOUT

2 lbs. pork, cut in 1½-inch cubes
1½ c. chopped onion
¾ c. butter
1 t. caraway seed
2 t. marjoram
   Grated rind of 1 lemon
1 clove garlic
1 T. paprika
4 c. water or stock

Sauté onion in butter. Mash caraway seed, marjoram, lemon rind, garlic and paprika in a mortar and add to onion. Stir in water and pork. Bring to a boil. Simmer, covered, for 1½ hours. Garnish with strips of red and green pepper. Serves 6.

MULLIGAN STEW

1 lb. beef, cubed
1 T. shortening
1 10½-oz. can tomato soup
1 t. salt
2 soup cans water
3 potatoes, cut in 4 pieces
3 carrots, sliced
2 onions, quartered

Brown meat in shortening. Add soup, salt and water. Cover tightly and simmer for 1 hour or until meat is tender. Add potatoes, carrots and onions; cover and simmer until liquid cooks down, about ½ hour. Add more water if needed while cooking. If stew is too thin, remove lid and simmer until thickened. Serves 4 to 6.

CHINESE STEW

1 lb. ground beef
1 stalk celery, thinly sliced
1 1-lb. can potatoes, drained
1 small onion, chopped
1 1-lb. can carrots, drained
1 10¾-oz. can undiluted vegetable soup
   Chow mein noodles

Brown ground beef, onion and celery. Drain fat. Add vegetables and soup. Simmer until celery is tender. Serve over chow mein noodles. Serves 4.

BEEF STEW

2 lbs. beef chuck, cut in 1½-inch cubes
2 T. vegetable oil
4 c. boiling water
1 t. lemon juice
1 t. Worcestershire sauce
1 clove garlic, optional
2 bay leaves
1 T. salt
½ t. pepper
½ t. paprika
   Dash allspice or cloves
1 t. sugar
4 carrots, diced
1 lb. small onions
2 c. potatoes, diced

In heavy kettle, brown meat in oil. Add water, lemon juice, Worcestershire sauce, garlic, bay leaves, salt, pepper, paprika, allspice, and sugar. Simmer for 2 hours. Add carrots, onions and potatoes. Cook until vegetables are tender and stew is thickened. Serves 4 to 6.

CAMPFIRE STEW

1½ sticks of butter or margarine
1½ lbs. onions, sliced or use frozen onion
1 t. caraway seed
1 small clove garlic, crushed
1 T. paprika
3 lbs. beef chuck or rump, cubed
1½ c. water
   Salt to taste
3 green peppers, seeded and cut in chunks

Melt butter in Dutch oven and simmer onions until tender and golden brown in color. Add seasonings. Add beef cubes and enough water to cover. Salt to taste. Cover and simmer gently until meat is tender. Add more water if necessary. Stir in green peppers during last half hour. Good served over noodles, rice or mashed potatoes. Serves 6 to 8.

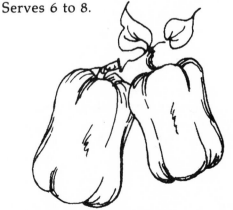

Seafood Soup

SALMON SOUP

1 1-lb. can pink salmon
8 c. cold water
1 1-lb. can tomatoes
2 c. chopped celery and leaves
½ c. chopped onion
2 t. salt
2 to 4 bay leaves
1 t. pepper
½ t. almond extract

Drain salmon. Discard bones, skin and dark meat areas. Break remainder into small pieces. Combine salmon with water, tomatoes, celery, onion and seasoning in a large soup kettle. Heat to boiling. Reduce heat and simmer, covered, for 30 minutes. Cool 10 minutes. Add almond extract. Serve immediately. Makes 3 quarts soup.

CLAM AND FISH SOUP

1 medium onion, chopped
2 carrots, thinly sliced
1 clove garlic, minced
3 T. vegetable oil
2 T. flour
   Salt and pepper to taste
1 8-oz. can tomato sauce
1 6½-oz. can minced clams
1 lb. frozen turbot, cut in 1-inch pieces

Sauté onion, carrots and garlic in oil until onion is tender. Stir in flour and seasonings. Add tomato sauce and 2 cups water. Bring to a boil. Add clams with liquid and turbot. Cover and simmer for about 30 minutes. Serves 4 to 6.

CREOLE FISH STEW

1 c. chopped onion
½ c. chopped green pepper
4 T. butter or margarine
1 1-lb. can whole tomatoes
1½ t. garlic salt
1 t. crumbled leaf thyme
1 10-oz. pkg. frozen succotash
2 pkgs. frozen cod fillets, cut
   in 2-inch lengths
½ t. salt
6 c. cooked rice

Sauté onion and green pepper in butter for 5 minutes. Stir in tomatoes, garlic salt and thyme. Simmer for 5 minutes, stirring often and breaking up tomatoes. Add succotash and cod. Add salt. Cover and simmer for 15 minutes or until fish flakes easily when tested with a fork. Serve stew over rice. Serves 6.

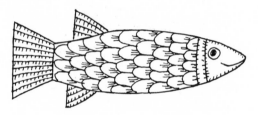

MANHATTAN CHOWDER

1 lb. fish fillet
½ c. chopped bacon
¼ c. chopped onion
¼ c. green pepper, chopped
1 c. celery, chopped
1 c. potatoes, diced
¼ t. thyme
1 t. salt
   Dash of cayenne pepper
2 c. tomato juice
1 4½-oz. can clams

Drain clams, reserving liquid. Add enough water to make 1 cup. Chop clams. Cut fish into ½-inch cubes. Fry bacon until lightly browned. Add onions, green pepper and celery. Cook until tender. Add liquid from clams. Add with potatoes and seasonings to bacon and onion mixture. Add fish and clams. Cook for 15 minutes or until potatoes are tender. Add tomato juice and heat. Serves 6.

50

Pictured opposite
Manhattan Chowd

CRAYFISH BISQUE

2 8-oz. crayfish or rock lobster tails, cleaned and minced
¼ c. butter or margarine
¼ c. flour
 Salt and pepper to taste
5 c. chicken broth
 Few drops Tabasco sauce
½ c. minced onion
1 leek, white part only
¼ c. chopped carrot
1 bay leaf
2 egg yolks
1 c. cream

Melt butter in large saucepan. Blend in mixture of flour, salt and pepper. Heat until mixture bubbles. Gradually stir in chicken broth and Tabasco sauce. Add vegetables and bay leaf. Heat to boiling. Cover. Simmer over low heat for 10 minutes. Remove bay leaf. Puree part of the crayfish and add to kettle. Simmer 10 minutes. Stir 3 tablespoons hot soup into beaten egg yolks. Return to pot. Cook for 5 minutes, stirring constantly. Do not boil. Add 1 cup cream. Stir to mix. Heat soup but do not boil. Serves 8.

MANHATTAN CLAM CHOWDER

1 c. chopped onion
⅔ c. finely chopped celery
2 t. finely chopped green pepper
1 clove garlic, minced
2 T. butter or margarine
1 large potato, diced
3 c. hot water
3 fresh tomatoes, peeled, seeded and diced
 or 1 1-lb. can tomatoes, chopped
1 pt. freshly opened clams, minced
 or 2 8-oz. cans minced clams
2 t. salt
¼ t. pepper
½ leaf thyme, crumbled
 Dash cayenne pepper
1 t. minced parsley
3 or 4 soda crackers, coarsely crumbled

In heavy soup kettle, sauté onion, celery, green pepper and garlic in butter or margarine for 20 minutes. Add potato and water. Cook until potato is tender. Add tomatoes, clams and their juices, salt, pepper, thyme and cayenne. Bring to a boil. Simmer 10 minutes. Stir in parsley. Pour in soup tureen over crackers, or in soup bowls over crackers. Makes 6 servings.

MOCK TURTLE SOUP

2 T. butter
1 medium onion, chopped
1 stalk celery, diced
1 carrot, diced
2 lbs. beef, cooked and diced
2 T. flour
2 c. beef stock
2 c. milk
4 hard-cooked eggs, chopped
 Salt and pepper to taste

Melt butter in heavy soup kettle. Add onions, celery and carrot. Sauté until tender. Add meat and flour, stirring to mix well. Add stock and milk, stirring until it thickens. Simmer for 20 minutes. Add chopped eggs, salt and pepper. Serves 4 to 6.

WALLEYE SOUP

2 large carrots, diced
1 medium onion, chopped
2 T. chopped parsley
2 medium potatoes, diced
½ c. diced celery
1 c. tomatoes
3 or 4 lbs. walleye fillets, cut
  in 2-inch slices
½ t. marjoram
1 T. butter
4 c. water
½ t. salt

Cook vegetables in enough water to cover until tender. Combine fish, salt, marjoram, butter and 4 cups water. Simmer until tender. Add vegetables to fish and liquid. Serves 4.

FISH SOUP WITH FISH DUMPLINGS

2½ lbs. pike or other fish, cut in small pieces
5 c. water
1 t. salt
½ medium onion, chopped
¼ c. plus 2 T. butter
5 T. flour
15 shrimp
8 oysters
½ c. white wine
2 egg yolks
12 small fish dumplings (see
   Soup Accompaniments)

Combine bones with water, onion, and salt. Simmer for one hour to make fish bouillon. Strain. Add enough water to make 4 cups bouillon. Melt ½ cup butter in large stew kettle. Stir in flour and brown lightly. Pour in fish bouillon and simmer slowly for 15 minutes. In a separate pan, stew fish in 2 tablespoons butter until tender. Boil shrimp in water and remove from shells. Heat oysters in wine; remove to a side dish. Make fish dumplings and cook 10 minutes in wine. Place dumplings, fish, shrimp and oysters in soup tureen. Strain bouillon mixture. Add egg yolks and heat to boiling. Pour bouillon over ingredients in soup tureen. Serves 4 to 6.

RICH OYSTER STEW

2 c. milk
2 c. cream
1½ pts. oysters
⅓ c. butter or margarine
2 t. salt
⅛ t. pepper

Scald the milk and cream in a 2-quart saucepan and set aside. Drain and reserve liquid from oysters. Pick over them to remove any shell particles. In a saucepan, melt butter. Add oyster liquid and simmer for 3 minutes. Add oysters. Simmer until oysters are plump and the edges begin to curl. Stir oyster mixture into milk and cream. Add salt and pepper. Serve at once with oyster crackers. Serves 4 to 6.

CURRIED TUNA SOUP

1 7-oz. can tuna
1 10¼-oz. can vegetable soup
1 soup can milk
¼ t. curry powder
  Thin lemon slices for garnish

Heat soup and milk in a saucepan. Add tuna that has been drained and rinsed. Flake fish. Heat to boiling. Add curry powder. Ladle into soup bowls. Float lemon slice on each bowl. Serves 4.

SHRIMP MINESTRONE

2 10¼-oz. cans vegetable soup
1 10¼-oz. can bean soup
3 cans water
3 T. butter or margarine
4 slices French bread, toasted
  Grated Parmesan cheese
2 5¾-oz. cans shrimp

Combine soups and water in saucepan. Heat. Add shrimp and butter or margarine. Heat. Place toasted bread in each bowl. Ladle soup over bread. Sprinkle with cheese. Serves 4 to 6.

POTATO LEEK SOUP

6 c. sliced potatoes
2 c. sliced leeks, white part only
6 c. stock or water
6 bouillon cubes
1 c. evaporated milk
2 T. butter or margarine
2 t. salt
Dash of pepper

Cook potatoes, leeks and stock for 45 minutes or until very tender. Cool slightly. Puree in blender. Reheat. Add milk, butter, salt and pepper. If too thick, thin with more milk or more stock. Serve hot with small slice of crisp toast. Serves 6 to 8.

POTATO SCALLION SOUP

2 medium potatoes, diced
2 or 3 T. butter
2 scallions or small onions, chopped
4 c. water or stock
1 carrot, chopped
½ c. chopped soup greens, spinach or mustard greens
½ c. thin egg noodles
Salt and pepper to taste

Sauté potatoes and onions in melted butter until golden. Add to water or stock in soup kettle. Add carrot, soup greens and egg noodles. Simmer until all ingredients are tender. Season to taste. Serve with crusty bread. Serves 4.

CORN BISQUE

6 ears of corn
1 T. melted butter
2 t. flour
⅛ t. pepper
1 T. instant chicken bouillon
2 c. milk
1 t. sugar
Salt to taste

Cut corn from cobs. Cover cobs with cold water. Bring to a boil and simmer for 20 minutes. Strain. Reserve liquid. To 2 cups of the corn liquid, add corn. Simmer 15 minutes. Blend butter and flour. Add to corn with remaining ingredients. Bring to a boil, stirring constantly. Makes 1 quart corn bisque.

Vegetable Soup

PARSNIP SOUP

2 parsnips, sliced
1 T. butter
3 c. milk
Salt and pepper to taste
1 c. whipped cream
Dash of paprika

Boil parsnips in salted water until tender. Drain. Put through a potato ricer or blend until smooth. In saucepan, combine milk and parsnip pulp. Season with salt and pepper. Heat to boiling. Serve with a dollop of whipped cream on top of each serving. Sprinkle paprika on top of cream. Serves 6.

ALPHABET SOUP

4 c. stock, beef or chicken
1 onion, chopped
1 stalk celery, chopped
1 carrot, diced
1 c. alphabet pasta
1 T. parsley, minced
Salt and pepper to taste

In large soup kettle, combine stock and vegetables; simmer ½ hour. Add alphabet noodles and simmer 20 minutes or until noodles are tender. Add parsley and salt and pepper to taste. Serves 6.

MINUTE MUSHROOM SOUP

2½ c. milk
½ c. finely chopped onion
1 c. chopped fresh mushrooms
¼ t. salt
1 t. parsley flakes

Scald milk and onion in top of a double boiler over medium heat. Add mushrooms, salt and parsley. Over boiling water, cook for 20 minutes or until mushrooms are tender. Serve piping hot with parsley and oyster crackers. Serves 4.

red opposite
habet Soup

VEGETABLE SOUP

8 c. beef stock or water
3 carrots, diced
1 c. fresh string beans
1 turnip, diced
1 parsnip, diced
1 t. salt
1 c. chopped celery
2 onions, diced
1 c. peas
1 can tomato soup
¼ t. pepper

Bring stock or water to a boil in large soup kettle. Add vegetables, tomato soup, and seasonings. Reduce heat and simmer until vegetables are tender. Serve hot, with crackers. Serves 6.

VEGETABLE POTATO SOUP

4 c. beef stock
1 15-oz. can mixed vegetables, drained
1 16-oz. can whole white potatoes, drained and diced
1 medium onion, chopped
3 slices bacon, diced
1 c. French-fried onion rings
Salt and pepper to taste

Sauté bacon until light brown and crisp. Drain and set aside. Sauté onion in drippings until golden. Combine stock, onion and bacon in soup kettle. Add vegetables and potatoes. Simmer for 20 minutes to blend flavors. Season to taste. Heat onion rings under broiler. Use onion rings as garnish. Serves 6.

POTATO SOUP WITH SOUR CREAM

2 c. diced potato
1 large onion, thinly sliced
2 c. boiling water
1 t. salt
½ t. pepper
2 c. cream
1 t. parsley flakes
1 c. sour cream

Cook potatoes and onion in water until tender. Add salt, pepper, and cream. Heat, but do not boil. Add parsley. Spoon a dollop of sour cream on top of each bowl. Serves 4.

TOMATO PEANUT BUTTER SOUP

1 c. chopped ripe tomatoes
1 small carrot, diced
1½ c. stock
1 small onion, chopped
1 T. butter
1 T. flour
Salt to taste
¼ c. peanut butter

Combine tomatoes, carrots, onion and stock in a saucepan. Bring to a boil. Simmer 20 minutes. Cool slightly. Blend in a blender. Reheat. Blend flour and butter and add to soup. Simmer, stirring, until soup thickens. Just before serving, stir in peanut butter. Mix well. Serves 4.

OLD-FASHIONED POTATO AND ONION SOUP

4 medium potatoes, diced
4 medium onions, diced
2 c. milk
1 T. butter
1 t. salt
½ t. pepper
½ t. caraway seed

Combine potatoes and onions in soup kettle. Add water to cover, salt and pepper. Bring to a boil. Simmer for 20 minutes. Add milk. Heat to a boil. Add butter. Ladle into soup bowls. Sprinkle with caraway seeds, if desired. Serves 4.

EGGPLANT SOUP

2 medium eggplants
6 c. water
1 t. salt
1 T. flour
1 T. butter
¼ t. pepper
1 c. milk or cream

Pare and cut eggplant into small pieces. Put in salted water and soak for 30 minutes. Drain. Put in soup kettle. Add water and boil until tender. Add milk or cream. Thicken with flour rubbed into the butter. Simmer until thickened. Add seasoning. Serves 4 to 6.

CARROT SOUP

6 slices bacon
1 large onion, chopped
  Veal knuckle
2 leeks, chopped
2 sprigs parsley
2 sprigs celery leaves, chopped
2 cloves
6 peppercorns
¼ t. thyme
8 c. water
6 carrots, cut in 2-in. chunks
¼ c. rice
1 onion, finely minced
1 T. butter
½ c. cream
  Salt and pepper

In large soup kettle sauté bacon and onion. Add veal knuckle, leeks, parsley, celery leaves, cloves, peppercorns and thyme. Add water and simmer for 3 to 4 hours. Strain the stock. Cook carrots, rice, and onion in the stock until carrots are tender. Force vegetables through a sieve or blend. Add pureed vegetables, butter, cream, salt and pepper to stock. Simmer for ½ hour. Serve over fried croutons. Serves 6.

CASHEW CARROT SOUP

4 T. vegetable oil
2 medium onions, sliced
2 c. shredded cabbage, turnip greens or chard
2 c. grated carrots
1 c. chopped apple
5 c. beef or vegetable stock
2 T. tomato paste
⅓ c. raw brown rice
½ c. coarsely chopped cashew nuts
½ c. raisins, optional
  Salt and pepper to taste
1 to 1½ c. yogurt for garnish

In a heavy soup kettle, sauté onions in oil. Stir in cabbage and sauté until tender. Add carrots, apple, beef stock and tomato paste. Bring mixture to a boil. Add rice. Simmer, covered, for 35 minutes or until carrots and rice are tender. Add cashew nuts and raisins. Steam until raisins are plump. Serve topped with a generous dollop of yogurt. Serves 4 to 6.

PEANUT SOUP

2 T. butter or margarine
5 green onions including tops, trimmed and sliced
1 celery stalk, minced
3 T. flour
1 10¾-oz. can chicken broth
2 c. milk
½ c. cream-style peanut butter
1½ t. lemon juice
⅛ t. liquid red pepper seasoning, optional
¼ c. chopped roasted peanuts for garnish
2 T. minced chives for garnish

Sauté green onions and celery in melted butter for 12 to 15 minutes or until tender. Blend in flour. Slowly add chicken broth and milk, stirring constantly until thickened. Strain soup. Puree onions and celery in blender. Combine puree with soup in kettle and reheat. Beat in peanut butter. Add lemon juice and seasonings. Heat, stirring occasionally for 15 to 20 minutes. Do not boil. Top individual servings with chopped peanuts and minced chives. Serves 6.

CHICKEN AND AUTUMN VEGETABLE SOUP

8 c. chicken broth or stock, fat skimmed off
2 medium onions, coarsely chopped
½ c. diced celery
2 T. minced parsley
1 t. thyme
1 bay leaf, crumbled
1 ½-in. strip lemon rind
4 c. canned tomatoes
2 c. dried corn or 2 c. whole kernel corn
1 lb. okra, sliced ½-in. thick
1 t. salt
⅛ t. pepper
2 c. hot fluffy rice

Combine chicken broth, onions, celery, parsley, thyme, bay leaf, lemon rind, tomatoes and dried corn in a very large, heavy kettle. Cover and simmer slowly about 1½ hours or until corn is tender. Add okra and simmer 10 to 15 minutes or until okra is tender. Add salt and pepper to taste. Stir in rice and let simmer uncovered for another 5 to 10 minutes. Serves 10 to 12.

Soup Accompaniments

CARROT DUMPLINGS

1 c. flour
2 t. baking powder
½ t. salt
3 T. shortening
½ c. milk
¼ c. shredded carrot
1 t. parsley flakes

Sift together flour, baking powder, and salt. Cut in shortening. Add in milk, carrot and parsley, stirring until flour is moist. Drop dumplings into simmering liquid in 8 mounds. Cover. Simmer 15 minutes without lifting cover. Serves 8.

FISH DUMPLINGS

1 c. chopped, cooked fish
1 egg white, beaten
½ c. bread crumbs
1 t. butter
½ t. minced parsley
1 t. salt

Thoroughly mix together all ingredients. Form into 2-inch balls. Steam for 10 minutes, covered, in broth or white wine. Serves 8.

PARSLEY DUMPLINGS

1 c. flour
1½ t. baking powder
1 t. chili powder
½ t. salt
1 T. minced parsley
2 T. shortening
½ c. milk

Sift together the flour, baking powder, chili powder and salt. Cut in shortening until mixture is like coarse meal. Add milk all at once. Mix lightly, until dough holds together. Drop into boiling liquid from rounded teaspoons. Simmer uncovered for 10 minutes. Cover and simmer 10 minutes longer to fluff up the dumplings. Serves 8.

MASHED POTATO DUMPLINGS

1½ c. flour
1 t. salt
1 t. baking powder
2 eggs, beaten
½ c. milk
2 c. mashed potatoes
1 c. bread crumbs
1 c. croutons, optional

Sift together flour, salt and baking powder. Add eggs, milk, potatoes and bread crumbs. Add croutons, if used. Form into 2-inch balls. Drop into rapidly boiling salted water. Cook for 15 minutes without lifting lid. Makes 12 dumplings.

DROP DUMPLINGS

1 c. flour
1½ t. baking powder
⅓ c. milk
½ t. salt
1 egg, beaten

Sift together flour, baking powder and salt and set aside. Combine egg and milk. Add to dry ingredients, mixing well. Drop by teaspoons into hot chicken broth. Cover and simmer 10 to 15 minutes. Do not lift cover during cooking.

LIVER DUMPLINGS

1 small onion, minced
½ t. butter
1 lb. liver
1½ T. suet
1½ t. salt
¼ t. pepper
¾ c. stale bread
2 eggs, beaten
1 t. parsley
Dash nutmeg
⅔ c. flour

Sauté onion in butter until golden. Set aside. Wipe liver and put through the meat grinder with suet. Add salt and pepper. Soften bread in water to cover. Squeeze dry. Add to liver. Add eggs, parsley, nutmeg and onion. Add flour gradually so that the mixture will hold together. Drop by tablespoons into boiling salted water. Cook, uncovered, for 10 minutes. Cover and cook for an additional 10 minutes. Makes 12 dumplings. Serve in hot beef broth.

Pictured opposite
Carrot Dumplings and Liver Dumpling

POTATO DUMPLINGS

4 potatoes, grated
8 slices of bread
  Water
1 small onion, grated
  Salt and pepper
2 eggs, well beaten
1 t. minced parsley

Dip bread in water and squeeze out most of the water. Combine all ingredients. Mix and form into 2-inch balls. Roll in flour. Drop in salted boiling water. Cook, covered, for 15 minutes.

SPONGE BALLS

2 eggs, separated
  Milk
1 c. flour
½ t. salt
2 t. melted butter

Add enough milk to egg whites to make one cup. Combine egg whites and milk, flour and melted butter in saucepan. Over moderate heat stir until batter is thick and smooth. Set aside to cool. Add egg yolks and salt. Mix well. Drop into bubbling soup by small teaspoons. Simmer, covered, for 8 minutes. Serve at once. Serves 6.

CHICKEN QUENELLES
OR DUMPLINGS

½ lb. chicken breast, raw
⅓ c. light or heavy cream
3 eggs
¼ t. salt
¼ t. white pepper
⅛ t. *each* mace, cloves, nutmeg and thyme

Grind chicken breast. In electric blender, puree all ingredients until smooth. Refrigerate for 1 hour. Fill a large saucepan ¾ full of lightly salted water. Bring to a boil; reduce heat to a simmer. Wet 2 teaspoons in hot water. Scoop out spoonfuls of chicken mixture with 2 spoons dipped in hot water. Drop into water. Remoisten spoons before shaping each dumpling. Steam dumplings 3 to 5 minutes. To keep warm, leave in water but remove from heat. Serve within 30 minutes in hot soup or broth.

FARINA DUMPLINGS

1 c. milk
½ c. farina
1 T. butter
½ t. salt
2 eggs, separated
  Dash of nutmeg

Bring milk to a boil. Add farina and simmer over low heat until it thickens. Add butter and salt. Cool slightly. Gradually add beaten egg yolks. Fold in stiffly beaten egg whites and nutmeg. Roll into small balls the size of marbles. Drop into boiling soup stock and cook, covered, for 10 minutes. Makes 12 dumplings.

SPINACH DUMPLINGS

1½ c. chopped spinach, cooked
2 c. flour
4 t. baking powder
½ t. salt
1 egg, well beaten
¼ c. milk
1 onion slice

Sift flour, baking powder and salt. Add egg and milk. Roll into thin dough. Cut into 3 or 4 inch squares. Into center of each square place 1 tablespoon well-seasoned spinach. Fold dough over and pinch edges. Drop dumplings into boiling water and add slice of onion. Cook, covered, for 15 minutes.

BREAD DUMPLINGS

2 T. butter
3 slices bread, cubed
2 T. melted butter
3 eggs, well beaten
2¼ c. milk
4½ c. flour
½ t. salt

In skillet, melt half the butter. Sauté bread cubes until golden brown. Set aside to cool. Blend melted butter with eggs and milk. Stir in salt and flour. Beat well. Let stand for 30 minutes. Form dough around bread cubes, shaping into small dumpling. Drop dumpling into 3 quarts rapidly boiling salted water. Cover and steam 15 to 20 minutes. Serve with soup.

EGG THREADS

2 eggs
2 T. sherry
Dash of salt
1 T. butter

Beat the eggs lightly with the sherry and salt. Melt butter in skillet. Slowly pour egg mixture into skillet, tipping it from side to side, spreading mixture thinly and evenly. Cook over low heat until set and the edge curls away from the pan. Invert on a plate. Cool and cut into narrow strips 2 inches long and 1/8 inch wide. Use with minced scallions as garnish for soup.

VEAL QUENELLES

1 lb. veal, twice ground
1¾ c. fresh bread crumbs
2 eggs, lightly beaten
1½ T. minced scallions
1½ T. grated Parmesan cheese
1½ T. minced parsley
1 t. salt
Dash nutmeg
Pepper to taste
6 c. hot clear soup

Combine all ingredients, mixing well. Using two teaspoons dipped into cold water, shape veal mixture into ovals. Drop into hot clear soup and steam for 8 minutes. Serve in soup. Makes about 48 quenelles.

LIVER NOODLES
(LEBERKNOEDEL)

1 lb. liver
1 onion, minced
1 T. butter
Salt and pepper to taste
2 eggs, well beaten
½ c. bread crumbs
¼ t. cloves
¼ t. marjoram

Simmer liver in water for 30 minutes. Drain. Grind liver fine. Add onion, butter, seasonings, and eggs. Work in bread crumbs to make a paste. Form into balls. Drop balls in bubbling soup and steam, covered, for 15 minutes. Serves 6 to 8.

GREEN NOODLES
(PASTA VERDE)

¼ lb. cooked spinach, chopped finely
3 c. flour
½ t. salt
3 eggs

Sift flour and salt. Make well in the center. Add eggs, one at a time, and mix thoroughly. Add spinach and mix well. Divide dough into half. Roll out on floured board 1/8 inch thick. Let stand for 1 hour. Roll up like jelly roll and cut in ¼-inch widths. Unroll and let dry 2½ hours. Prepare other half of dough same way. Drop into boiling water or broth and cook until tender.

HOMEMADE NOODLES

2 eggs
1 t. salt
2 T. water
2 c. flour

Beat eggs until light. Add salt and water. Work in flour to make a very stiff dough. Knead; then form into a ball. Roll out on floured board until very thin. Dust top with additional flour and roll up like jelly roll. Cut in desired widths. Spread out on flat surface and let dry two hours. Drop in boiling chicken broth. Makes 6 cups noodles.

SPAETZLE

3¼ c. flour
1 t. salt
½ t. nutmeg
4 eggs, slightly beaten
½ c. milk
8 c. boiling salted water
¼ c. butter or margarine

Combine flour, salt and nutmeg. Stir in eggs and milk. Beat for 2 minutes until smooth. Makes a soft batter. Pour batter into a large-holed sieve, colander, food mill or potato ricer. Hold sieve directly over boiling water and force batter through with a wooden spoon. Cook 6 to 8 minutes, stirring occasionally. Drain well. Melt butter in a heavy skillet. Add spaetzle to hot butter. Sauté quickly for 2 or 3 minutes until golden. Serve hot with Hungarian goulash. Serves 8.

61

SEASONED CROUTONS

4 slices bread
  Butter
¼ t. garlic powder *or* seasoned salt

Generously butter both sides of the bread. Sprinkle with garlic powder or seasoned salt. Cut into ½-inch cubes. Bake 10 to 15 minutes stirring occasionally, until golden brown and crisp. Cubed bread can be fried in seasoned butter, stirring until browned.

FRANKFURTER CRISPS

4 frankfurters, diagonally sliced into ½-inch strips
¼ c. flour
1 egg white, lightly beaten
½ c. dry bread crumbs
  Vegetable oil

Dust sliced frankfurters with flour. Dip them in egg whites and coat with dry bread crumbs. Fry in hot deep oil at 375°, turning frankfurters until golden brown. Drain on paper towel. Makes about 40 crisps.

TINY BAKING POWDER BISCUITS

2 c. flour
3 t. baking powder
1 t. salt
¼ c. shortening
¼ c. milk

Preheat oven to 450°. Sift together flour, salt and baking powder. Cut in shortening until mixture looks like course meal. Stir in milk and mix to make a soft dough. Turn dough out on floured board. Knead 20 to 25 times. Roll ½ inch thick. Cut with 2-inch biscuit cutter. Bake on ungreased baking sheet for 10 minutes. Serve with soup or stew.

CHEESE THINS

1 c. flour
½ t. salt
¼ t. paprika
    Pinch cayenne pepper
¾ c. grated sharp Cheddar cheese
6 T. butter
2 T. grated Parmesan cheese
¼ c. cold beer
1 egg yolk
2 T. beer

Sift together the flour, salt, paprika and cayenne. Add Cheddar cheese, butter and Parmesan cheese, mixing well. Add beer and roll dough into a cylinder about 1 inch in diameter. Wrap dough in foil and freeze for 1 hour. Slice dough into ⅛-inch thick rounds. Place on a baking sheet, 1 inch apart. Brush rounds with an egg wash made by beating 1 egg yolk with 2 tablespoons beer. Sprinkle with caraway or poppy seed. Bake in 450° oven for 12 to 14 minutes or until lightly browned. Makes about 36 thins.

PIMIENTO WHIPPED CREAM

½ c. heavy cream, whipped
½ c. minced pimiento
1 T. lemon juice
2 t. minced chives
    Salt and pepper to taste

Fold pimiento, lemon juice, chives and seasoning into whipped cream. Makes about 1 cup. Serve afloat on cold soups.

LITTLE HATS FOR SOUP

2 c. flour
½ t. salt
2 eggs
3 T. cold water

In large bowl, sift together flour and salt. Make a well in center of the flour and mix in the eggs and water. Mix well into a stiff dough. Turn out on floured board. Knead. Roll out dough to ⅛-inch thickness. Cut with 2½-inch cookie cutter. Place ½ teaspoon of mixture in the center of each round. Moisten edges of pasta with water. Fold each round in half, covering the mound of filling. Press edges together to seal. Drop in hot broth and cook 20 to 25 minutes or until pasta is tender. Test tenderness by pressing pasta against edges of the pan with spoon or fork. Makes about 30 pastas.

FILLING

½ c. Ricotta or cottage cheese
½ c. finely chopped cooked chicken
2 T. grated Parmesan cheese
1 egg, beaten
⅛ t. salt
⅛ t. nutmeg

Combine all ingredients and mix well.

SODA CRACKERS

2 c. flour
1 t. salt
½ t. baking soda
¼ c. butter
½ c. buttermilk
1 egg

Sift together flour, salt and soda. Cut in butter. Stir in buttermilk and egg mixing until liquid is absorbed. Knead dough for 5 minutes on lightly floured board. Roll out half of the dough into a rectangle ⅛ inch thick. Place on a buttered baking sheet. With a fluted pastry wheel perforate dough in 2-inch squares. Prick dough with a fork. Bake in 400° oven for 12 to 14 minutes or until lightly browned. Break squares apart and transfer to a rack to cool. Prepare and bake remaining dough the same way. Store crackers in an airtight container. Makes 60 crackers.

INDEX